MERCANTILE CREDITS AND COLLECTIONS

THE MACMILLAN COMPANY
NEW YORK · BOSTON · CHICAGO · DALLAS
ATLANTA · SAN FRANCISCO

MACMILLAN & CO., LIMITED
LONDON · BOMBAY · CALCUTTA
MELBOURNE

THE MACMILLAN CO. OF CANADA, LTD.
TORONTO

MERCANTILE CREDITS AND COLLECTIONS

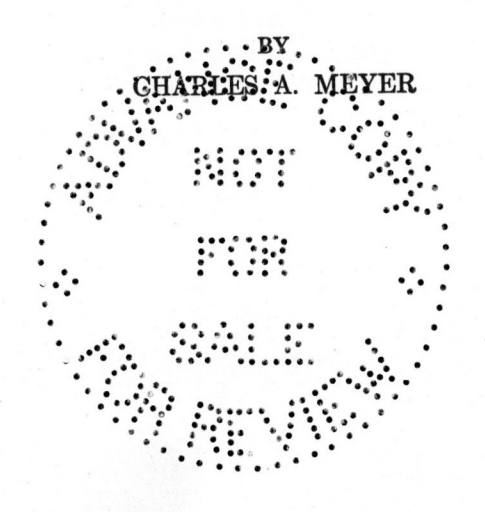

BY

CHARLES A. MEYER

New York
THE MACMILLAN COMPANY
1919

All rights reserved

COPYRIGHT, 1919,
By THE MACMILLAN COMPANY.

Set up and electrotyped. Published July, 1919.

PREFACE

In this volume the author has attempted to discuss one branch of the various classes of credit, that is, mercantile credit, and the methods to be pursued in making mercantile collections, and has taken a view of the collection feature of mercantile credits from a practical standpoint, based on experience, and without strict regard to the theoretical application or analysis of all phases of credit.

There are two general classes of credit—public credit and private credit—but political economists usually divide credit into five classes: mercantile, personal, banking, public and investment credit. This volume makes reference to mercantile credit only, no attempt being made to discuss the other branches of credit classes.

The suggestions offered are based upon practical experience, and the book is intended for credit men and for those interested in the subject of mercantile credit generally from a practical business standpoint.

CHAS. A. MEYER.

Chicago, Ill.
October, 1918

CONTENTS

	PAGE
INTRODUCTORY	ix

PART I

MERCANTILE CREDIT

CHAPTER I

The Credit System and the Fundamental Principles of Credit

Greater Factor than Money in Development of World—Supplying the Place of Money—Function of Banks in Liquidating Credit—Open Book Account System—Conditional Sales Contracts as Credit Instruments—Promissory Notes—Trade Acceptances—Character and Honesty—Reciprocal Faith—Business Ability—Ability to Pay—Practical Business Experience—General Reputation—Sound Business Judgment.................................... 3

CHAPTER II

Functions of the Credit Man

Position of Trust and Responsibility—Safeguarding Property and Investments of Employer—Avoiding Losses by Collecting and Weighing Facts—Constructive Methods—Training Salesmen—Increasing Sales by His Own Efforts—Business Advisor of Customers—Getting Confidence of Customers—Discouraging Dishonesty................. 12

Chapter III

Sources of Information, and Forms, Suggested, to be Obtained from Salesmen

Teaching Salesmen in the Art of Obtaining Credit Information—Advantages of Obtaining Complete Credit Reports from Salesmen—Salesmen's Form upon which to Report Merchants, Fully Analyzed—Salesmen's Report for Manufacturers—Salesmen's Report for Farmers—Salesmen's Report for Oil Producers—Salesmen's Report for Metal Mining Companies................................ 19

Chapter IV

Sources of Information, and Forms, Suggested, Exclusive of Those from Salesmen

Advantage of Obtaining Signed Statement Direct from Customer—Advantage of Using Special Blanks with Self-contained Envelope—Form to be Used in Obtaining Statements Direct from Customers—Form to be Used in Seeking Information from Banks—Form to be Used in Seeking Information from Other Merchants—Obtaining Reports from Mercantile Agencies—Obtaining Information from Attorneys... 39

Chapter V

Method of Compiling Information and Final Disposition of Orders

Filing Reports in Credit Folders—Keeping Reports in Date Order—Revising Credit Files Periodically—How to Fix and Change Credit Limits—Card System on Credit Limits—Assistance of Bookkeeper—Record of Declined Credits—Record of Approved but Unshipped Orders—Letters of Acceptance—Forming Good Impressions First—Sending

CONTENTS ix

PAGE

Copies of Acceptances to Salesmen—Approving Orders—Temporary Approval in the Interest of Service—Phraseology of Letters Declining Orders—Keeping Records of Declined Orders...................................... 46

Chapter VI

Co-operation and Diplomacy

Basis of Mutuality—How to Win the Confidence of Salesmen, in Various Ways—Lining up the Customer Fully Explained—Advantages of Co-operation—Co-operation with Banks—Removing Prejudices of Other Merchants and Competitors—Co-operation at Creditors' Meetings—Problem of Declining an Order—Profitable to Have Good Will of Customer even if Credit is Refused—Style of Letters to be Used in Turning Down Orders—Essential to Keep Good Will of Salesmen even when Orders from Poor Risks are Declined—Benefit of Credit Man Visiting the Territory.. 52

Chapter VII

Converting Doubtful Orders into Good Ones, and the Use of Guarantees

Diplomatic Use of Suggestion—Getting the Cash by Tact—How to Approach a Buyer for Security—Securing the Personal Guarantee of Individuals for Corporate Purchases—Undertaking of Relatives—Backing of Landlord to Tenant—Other Personal Relations—Form of Guarantee Recommended by National Association of Credit Men—Must be in Legally Binding Form—Consideration Must Be Ample—Guarantees on New and on Old Accounts Require Different Considerations—Method of Avoiding All Question of Consideration for Guarantee on Obligation Already Owing—Form to be Used for Guarantee on Debt Already Owing... 66

Chapter VIII

How to Read a Financial Statement

Close Analysis Necessary—Age of Individuals a Factor—Established versus New Corporations—Segregating Quick Assets and Quick Liabilities—Contingent Liabilities a Consideration—Proportion of Assets to Liabilities Discussed—Bank Loans a Large Factor—Loans from Others than Banks—Intangible Assets—Conservatives versus Speculators—Market for Product—General Prosperity of the Community—Fire, Life, Workmen's Compensation, and Public Liability Insurance—Determining the Turnover.. 75

Chapter IX

Conditional Sales Contracts

Definition of—Their Effect, and Advantages to the Buyer—General Exceptions to Their Validity—When they may be Used to Advantage—Distinction between Recording and Filing—Criminal Liability for Disposing of Property before Payment Discussed—Remedies on Default of Buyer—Election of Remedies—Tendency of Courts to Protect Buyer—Training Salesmen to be Careful—Essential to Know if Individual can Bind Corporate Buyer—Form of Agreement Must Be so Full and Complete as to Cover all Circumstances.. 82

Chapter X

Trade Acceptances

Overcoming Prejudices—Definition of—Function of, compared with Promissory Notes—Advantages to Seller—Advantages to Banker—Quickens the Turnover—Advantages to the Buyer—Reducing Losses......................... 89

Chapter XI

General Knowledge of Law, and Information on Credit Conditions

Knowledge of Certain Specified Subjects Helpful—Practical Operation of the Law—Guiding Lawyers by Definite Instructions—Knowledge of Implied Warranties—Contingent Damages—Redemption Laws—Sources of General Legal Information—Factors that Disturb Credits—Sources of Information on Financial Conditions—Study of Crop Conditions—Sources of Information on Crop Conditions—Information on Trade and Industrial Conditions—Information on Mining and Oil Industries—General Local Conditions... 97

PART II

MERCANTILE COLLECTIONS

Chapter I

Functions of a Good Collector

Getting the Money when Due—Making Few Enemies—Constructive Methods—Careful Analyses—Getting the Debtor's Confidence—Granting Extensions only for Adequate Consideration—Adjusting Complaints—Partial Collections on Disputed Claims—Monthly Statements—Advantages of Itemizing—Notices of Maturity of Notes—Contract Payments—Special Letter Notices—Draft against Bill of Lading—Trade Acceptance Notice.................... 107

Chapter II

Follow-up System, and Collection Letters

System Necessary to Persistency—Holding Good Will of Debtors—Classifying Monthly Statements—Follow-up Dates in Files—Card System—Collection Letters—Special List of Old Accounts—Maturities of Notes—Avoiding Form Letters—Delivering Your Message—Attracting Attention in the Opening Statement—Effective Letters—Using Pretexts—Positive Attitude—Use of Suggestion—Distinctive Letters.. 114

Chapter III

Unusual, Unique and Resourceful Methods

Foresight—The Principle of Security—When to Convert Open Book Accounts into Promissory Notes—Dealing with Contentious Debtors—How to Collect Attorneys' Fees from the Debtor—Form of Promissory Note Recommended—Printed Waiver of Protest on Notes—Collateral Notes—Unusual Forms of Collateral Security Recommended—Cutting off Debtor's Equity of Redemption by Using Special Form of Collateral Note Recommended—How to Use Open Book Accounts of Debtor as Security—Form of Assignment of Open Book Accounts—Procedure of Using Notes Due Debtor as Security—When and How to Get Postdated Checks—Procedure of Collecting Checks Dishonored because of Insufficient Funds—Effective Method of Collecting Small Past Due Accounts—Form of Blank Check and Stub Recommended—Charging Interest—Obtaining Individual Guarantee of Payment—Use of Registered Mail—Special Delivery Letters—Collecting by Telegraph—Creating Offsets—Reciprocity—How to Collect from Precarious and Contrary Debtors—Tracing the Lost Ones—Rule to Follow on Default of Payment.......... 121

Chapter IV

Commercial Arbitration—Adjustment Bureaus—Collection Agencies

Advantages of Arbitration—Procedure Followed in Settlement of Arbitrated Controversies, Including Agreement for Entry of Judgment—Suggesting Arbitration to Attorneys

CONTENTS xiii

—Arbitration Committees of the Chicago Association of Commerce—Outline of Aims and Objects—Controlling Receivers—Appraisers and Trustees—Prosecutions—Competent Administration of Estates—Methods of Procedure—Creditors' Committees—Results Accomplished—Time to Place Accounts—Selecting the Agency—Keeping Records of Results—Getting Accurate Reports of Status of Claims—How to Properly Place Claims for Collection.... 141

Chapter V

Bankruptcy

Knowledge of Practical Operation of Law—Theory of the Law—Correcting Mistaken Practices—Advantages of Law to Creditors—Its Primary Object—Care in Filing Creditors' Claims—Voting for a Trustee—Kind of Trustee to Select—Functions of a Trustee—Analysis of Preferences—Difficulties Encountered in Recovering on Preferences to Estate—Status of Conditional Sales in Bankruptcy Court.. 152

Chapter VI

Your Own Collection Agency. Organization—Collection Letters—Methods

Plan Fully Outlined—No Expense Involved—Greater Efficiency in Collections—Maintaining Your Own Control of Obligations—Forms of Articles of Incorporation—Suitable Name—Proper Address—Avoiding Special Fee in States Where Special License is Required from a Collection Agency—Designing the Proper Letterhead—Demands—Threats—Persuasive Letters—Collecting in Installments—Advertising Obligations for Sale—Posting Notices in Debtor's Neighborhood—Offering Claim to Debtor's Bank—Use of the Mourning Envelope—Placing Claims with Attorneys for a Suit—Examining Judgment Debtors—Dealing with Foreign Attorneys................................. 164

PART III

UNITED STATES BANKRUPTCY LAW

Chapter I

Definitions

Meaning of Words and Phrases............................ 179

Chapter II

Creation of Courts of Bankruptcy and Their Jurisdiction

Courts and Jurisdiction................................... 183

Chapter III

Bankrupts

Acts of Bankruptcy—Who May Become Bankrupts—Partners—Exemption of Bankrupts—Duties of Bankrupts—Death or Insanity of Bankrupts—Protection and Detention of Bankrupts—Extradition of Bankrupts—Suits by and against Bankrupts—Compositions, When Confirmed—Compositions, When Set Aside—Discharges, When Granted—Discharges, When Revoked—Co-debtors of Bankrupts—Debts not Affected by Discharge....................... 187

Chapter IV

Courts and Procedure Therein

Process, Pleadings, and Adjudications—Jury Trials—Oaths, Affirmations—Evidence—Reference of Cases After Adjudication—Jurisdiction of United States and State Courts—Jurisdiction of Appellate Courts—Appeals and Writs of Error—Arbitration of Controversies—Compromises—Designation of Newspapers—Offenses—Rules, Forms, and Orders—Computation of Time—Transfer of Cases...... 202

Chapter V

Officers, Their Duties and Compensation

PAGE

Creation of Two Offices—Appointment, Removal and Districts of Referees—Qualifications of Referees— Oath of Office of Referees—Number of Referees—Jurisdiction of Referees—Duties of Referees—Compensation of Referees—Contempts before Referees—Records of Referees—Referee's Absence or Disability—Appointment of Trustees—Qualifications of Trustees—Death or Removal of Trustees—Duties of Trustees—Compensation of Trustees—Accounts and Papers of Trustees—Bonds of Referees and Trustees—Duties of Clerks—Compensation of Clerks and Marshals—Duties of Attorney General—Statistics of Bankruptcy Proceedings............................ 214

Chapter VI

Creditors

Meetings of Creditors—Voters at Meetings of Creditors—Proof and Allowance of Claim—Notice to Creditors—Who May File and Dismiss Petitions—Preferred Creditors........ 231

Chapter VII

Estates

Depositories for Money—Expenses of Administering Estates—Debts Which May Be Proved—Debts Which Have Priority—Declarations and Payments of Dividends—Unclaimed Dividends—Liens—Set-offs and Counterclaims—Possession of Property—Title to Property—Clerks to Keep Indexes—Extra Fees Forbidden.......................... 241

Appendix

Requirements of Each State as to Conditional Sales Contracts

	PAGE
Alabama	255
Arizona	255
Arkansas	256
California	256
Colorado	256
Connecticut	256
Delaware	257
District of Columbia	257
Florida	257
Georgia	258
Idaho	258
Illinois	259
Indiana	259
Iowa	259
Kansas	260
Kentucky	260
Louisiana	260
Maine	261
Maryland	261
Massachusetts	261
Michigan	262
Minnesota	262
Mississippi	262
Missouri	263
Montana	264
Nebraska	264
Nevada	264
New Hampshire	265
New Jersey	265
New Mexico	265
New York	266
North Carolina	266
North Dakota	266
Ohio	267

	PAGE
Oklahoma	267
Oregon	267
Pennsylvania	268
Rhode Island	268
South Carolina	268
South Dakota	269
Tennessee	269
Texas	269
Utah	270
Vermont	270
Virginia	270
Washington	271
West Virginia	271
Wisconsin	271
Wyoming	272

Forms of Conditional Sales Contracts

Short Form, Conditional Sale Contract	273
Simple Form of Conditional Sale	274
Pennsylvania Lease Form of Contract	275
Machinery Form of Conditional Sale Contract	277
Form of Contract Used in Selling Engines	281
Short Order Form, Conditional Sale Contract, for Salesmen	289
Conditional Contract of Sale	291

INTRODUCTORY

Most credit men and collectors must obtain their knowledge through years of practical business experience, as most books heretofore published on the subject or credits and collections are largely theoretical, well written by authorities on political economy, but not based upon actual experience in that line of work. For this reason it seems desirable to treat mercantile credits and collections from actual experience and an attempt has been made to do this in this volume.

The author has been brief and has kept from going into exhaustive detail as much as possible, so that a broad vision of the subject may be obtained without finding the reading of the subject-matter burdensome. It is the purpose in compiling the work to influence the reader to use constructive thought in connection with what is herein stated.

After understanding and absorbing the fundamental principles of credit and the function of credit grantors, stress is laid upon the obtaining of reliable and accurate information, followed by the use of calm and deliberate judgment, and if this general procedure is followed, regardless of the policy of a business institution, the losses will be less by a study and analysis of the application of the methods or principles outlined in the first part of the book on mercantile credits; and if the judgment of the reader has failed him in the granting of credit or subsequent unforeseen difficulties have later arisen, an exhaustive search of the existing facts, coupled with the same careful analysis and deliberate application of the principles or suggestions in Part II on mercantile collections will still enable him to avoid losses that would otherwise occur.

PART I
MERCANTILE CREDIT

MERCANTILE CREDITS AND COLLECTIONS

CHAPTER I

THE CREDIT SYSTEM AND THE FUNDAMENTAL PRINCIPLES OF CREDIT

Credit has been a greater factor in the development and progress of the world than money. Had the development and progress of the world been limited to the use of money only this generation would now be in a state of development that existed centuries ago. Credit has stimulated labor, industry and commerce. A slight disturbance in the credit system is felt in every line of business, and its ramifications are such and its operations so internationally extensive that this disturbance reaches foreign business as well as domestic. Present-day commercial life would be demoralized if credit should cease.

Property is represented by hard money, which is the standard or measure of value, and hard money is represented equally as much by credit, and it so thoroughly supplies the place of money that in most commercial transactions the actual transfer of money from one party in a transaction to the other rarely ever takes place.

The banking system is probably the most highly developed and best regulated branch of the credit system. Practically all business operations are liquidated by the credit system through the medium of the banks, and to-day they are as much a clearing house of credit as they are a clearing house of money. However, as the subject to be dealt with in this book relates to mercantile credit only, no discussion of the system of banking credits will be undertaken.

Much of the business of this country is to-day done on credit through what is known as the Open Book Account System. Under this system a buyer places an order for merchandise, either verbally or in writing, which the seller fills, relying upon the promise and ability of the buyer to pay for the property at some future date. Often the promise to pay is merely implied. Orders are placed most generally without any definite promise to pay. The transaction is largely one of faith, supplemented by information the seller has as to the character, reputation, financial standing and ability of the buyer to pay.

Where salesmen are employed, the buyer's written order is usually obtained, and the terms of sale are shown on the order and a copy of the signed order is left with the buyer. If the character of the business does not make it practical to obtain written orders, or when a written order is received from a buyer by mail, the order should be acknowledged, so that there is no misunderstanding as to what is to be shipped and in order that the buyer's attention may be called to any discrepancy. A shipping ticket, or a charge ticket, is then made up, from which the goods are shipped, and an invoice is mailed to the customer and on the first of the month a statement of account is rendered. The buyer's duty is to check over the statement or bill, and if correct pay the amount shown, which is usually by check or draft. It is a remarkable tribute to the good faith of human nature and belief in our fellow being that there are not more losses in business under this loose system of open book account credits.

In some cases merchandise is sold under what is known as the Conditional Sales Contract. This enables the seller to retain title to the goods furnished until the purchase price has been paid by the buyer. Pianos, victrolas, machinery, farm implements, wagons and buggies, automobiles, sewing machines, and most mechanical devices sold on the installment plan are sold under the Conditional Sales Contract. Sellers of this class of merchandise usually require a cash payment with the order large enough to cover the wear and tear and depreciation in case they are compelled to take back the property because of default on the part of the buyer. A complete outline of the method of making sales under conditional sales contracts will be later outlined in a separate chapter.

In money transactions the extensions of credit is

usually represented by a promissory note, either secured or unsecured. The security may be collateral, such as stocks, bonds or other evidence of indebtedness, or may be in the form of a mortgage on real estate or personal property. For practical purposes, however, a distinction should be made in mercantile transactions between secured and unsecured notes, in that an unsecured note really represents credit based wholly upon the integrity and ability of the maker to pay, whereas a secured note is merely an evidence of indebtedness in which the ability, and frequently the integrity of the maker are not much of a factor, the holder of the paper relying upon the real estate or collateral pledged as assurance of ultimate payment, almost wholly regardless of the ability of the maker to pay the indebtedness from the proceeds or realization of trading in other assets.

Another instrument of mercantile credit is the trade acceptance. The most important function of the trade acceptance is to liquify open book accounts and make them available for discount at banks. As distinguished from a promissory note, which is a "promise to pay," a trade acceptance is an "order to pay" and is based entirely upon current transactions. The use of such instruments in this country is comparatively new and a separate chapter will be devoted to the subject.

Many contingencies often prevent the buyer from carrying out his obligation, and the following chapters point out the dangers, outline the methods and suggest some remedies for preventing losses which frequently could have been prevented if the seller had handled the situation properly.

One of the first requisites a buyer must have is character and honesty. It is often dangerous to extend credit to one who has all the other necessary requisites to enable him to pay; in fact, credit men must always be on the alert to prevent their employers from being defrauded by buyers who have the ability to pay but, lacking character and honesty, try to make it profitable to themselves by avoiding wherever possible the payment of their just debts. In a retail trade, for instance, much of the credit that is extended to buyers, particularly covering the necessities of life, is extended solely upon the character and honesty of the buyer.

Another fundamental attribute of credit is faith—faith on the part of the seller that the buyer can and will carry out his obligation with a reasonable degree of promptness and certainty; and faith upon the part of the buyer that the seller can and will deliver what he has contracted to deliver or agreed to deliver, within the time, and of a quality, agreed upon. This faith upon the part of the seller must extend further than a mere belief that the buyer can meet his obligations. It is the duty of the credit man to ascertain the facts that will make this faith tangible. The seller must have faith, not only in the character and honesty of the buyer, but in the business in which the buyer is engaged, and in his ability, experience and judgment. There are various sources through which this information can be obtained, which will be outlined in a separate chapter.

Ability of the buyer to pay is dependent upon many different factors, but most usually upon his solvency and resourcefulness. A resourceful debtor frequently extracts himself from facing bankruptcy by obtaining an extension from his creditors, which is usually granted if they have faith in the continued profitable operation of the business and eventual ability of the debtor to pay his obligations. To be what is commonly known as an "able business man" is, however, not sufficient. The ability of the buyer must be of a character such only as is developed by long experience in the particular line of business undertaken. The ability of a debtor to pay, also, frequently depends upon whether or not he has himself extended credit judicially and whether or not he can in turn collect from his debtors. His ability to pay may depend upon his having sufficient knowledge and judgment to be able to produce an article for which there is a profitable market, or, in the case of jobbers, to resell a commodity at a profit. The ability of the average wage earner or salaried employee to meet his obligations depends somewhat on the nature of his employment and to some extent on whether or not he is living beyond his means.

Another necessary factor of credit is experience. The

one to whom credit is extended must have had experience in the line of business in which they are engaged, and this experience in most cases must be practical and not theoretical. A school or business college cannot turn out young men as full-fledged business men who can make an immediate business success without any practical experience. A young man of immature experience may make a success of business and may be entitled to credit, if he has all the other necessary factors to establish a credit, but the hazard is greater in dealing with an inexperienced credit risk than it is in dealing with an experienced one.

Experience is also required on the part of the credit grantor, in that he must be able to analyze human nature and have had experience in dealing with business men and business institutions; he must have had some experience in analyzing financial statements; so that it is clear experience is a very necessary element of credit.

The general reputation of the parties to a transaction is also an important element of credit. If a seeker of credit has a poor reputation for paying his bills, or has the reputation of dissipating or neglecting his business, or has the reputation of a generally low moral standard, the credit man should carefully investigate his standing in this respect. Sometimes such a reputation is unjust, and has been circulated by enemies. In that sense reputation is different from character, for a man may have a poor reputation temporarily but fundamentally have a good character. On the other hand, clever seekers of credit have practically no character but often temporarily have a good reputation. A man's reputation, whether good or bad, always reflects upon his credit accordingly and his reputation is a large element of his credit.

Another element of credit is judgment. The use of the term "judgment" covers a broad field, but whether good, sound business judgment exists in a seeker of credit or not can usually be determined by proper inquiry. For instance, a manufacturer who is devoting a large part of his capital and labor toward experimenting in theoretical or visionary ways naturally affects his credit; a jobber who frequently overstocks displays poor judgment; a jobber who invests a large portion of his capital in a building frequently displays poor judgment. If the assets of a seeker of credit are tied up in slow-moving or non-productive assets, good business judgment is lacking. The business man of good judgment will see that his turn-over is frequent; that terms of sale are reasonably short; that he is not overstocked, and that his merchandise does not become obsolete. An individual who expects credit will display good judgment by not living beyond his means, so that his obligations can be paid when they are due. If he has any tendency to speculate, he should only speculate with certain funds from a savings account. Judgment must also be displayed on the part of the granter of credit. After careful inquiry of the buyer's standing and after weighing all the facts, the final approval or rejection of a credit order requires good judgment. Many doubtful looking orders can be made safe by applying the proper remedy as will be shown later herein.

CHAPTER II

FUNCTIONS OF THE CREDIT MAN

It is not sufficient for the credit man to merely O K the order of a concern rated AA A1 and turn down orders of buyers with merely medium or poor rating; an office boy or clerk could exercise that function. The credit man must not only get all the available reliable information that he can concerning a customer, but should also make an effort to turn an order from a poorly rated concern into a good order by obtaining security, or by giving advice to the customer or in any other way that he can. His position is one of trust and responsibility, and in many respects his responsibility is greater than that of a banker. The banker is very frequently in a position to obtain collateral or real estate security; he has the advantage of seeing a borrower's checking account, and is also in position to require a written, definite, concrete, unconditional obligation of the borrower before parting with value.

On the other hand, a credit man who is safeguarding the property and investments of his employer usually is furnished with nothing but the order of a buyer, which may be only verbal, but even if written is usually unsecured, and there is no definite, concrete obligation to pay on a certain date, other than a sort of general understanding on the part of the buyer of what the terms of the seller may be. Often a credit man must approve or reject such an order on very short notice, and has but a limited time to investigate the buyer's standing, and seldom has the opportunity of analyzing a buyer's personal characteristics from personal contact, an advantage, for instance, which a banker often has.

Notwithstanding these facts, it is not the function of a credit man to undertake to be a prophet or take a chance on some buyer. The function of a prophet is to determine a future probable event without having any known factors to guide him—a sort of mystic science. The function of a credit man is to determine a future probable event (that is, whether the buyer can and will pay on the day agreed upon) in a commercial transaction, based upon present KNOWN factors— an exact science.

The great difficulty is the tendency to attempt to determine this probable future commercial event without having all the present known factors as a guide; or by using as a guide information that has not been verified, and this is very frequently the cause of unusual and unnecessary losses that could have been avoided if the credit man had sufficiently investigated the facts; or if the credit man had so developed the other component parts of the organization with which he is connected to obtain these facts.

In the proper exercise of his duties the credit man can improve the business of his employers by constructive methods; he can guide the salesmen of the company by analyzing territorial conditions; he can give the salesman a list of good concerns in the community that the salesman intends to visit, instead of allowing the salesman to form his own conclusions in that regard. Many salesmen lack sufficient training in financial matters and often seek to establish an agency based wholly upon the physical appearance of the store and the look of prosperity of the prospective customer. Sometimes the best looking store in a community, the building and fixtures of which represent substantially all the capital of the concern, is on the verge of bankruptcy. Frequently the physical look of prosperity is due to overexpansion and overbuying, and in addition to the money invested in the building, the balance of their capital may be tied up in slow-moving assets. It is not, however, unusual for a salesman to rely largely upon the physical appearance of the prosperous looking individual and the prosperous looking establishment which he conducts, and usually when making an agency with this concern considers that he has made a desirable agency and is very much exercised if the credit man later rejects the order. In the same town there may be, and probably are, one or two other concerns whose business establishments are not so pretentious and whose more modest owners are somewhat less prosperous looking, but who are doing a good, conservative business, and who are paying their bills promptly and are in good credit standing.

Therefore, one of the functions of the credit man of an institution employing traveling salesmen is to properly guide the salesman starting out on the territory by giving him a list of desirable credit risks in each of the towns he will visit on his trip, in order that money will not be uselessly wasted in obtaining undesirable orders and in order that closer harmony may be established between the sales and financial organizations. This list can be readily compiled by reference to Dun's or Bradstreet's rating books.

The functions of the retail credit man present a somewhat different aspect. His clients are frequently prosperous looking but are poor credit risks. For instance, in clothing or dry goods establishments the moral risk is a large factor, and it is very rarely that a loss occurs in this class of trade if the moral hazard is good and the seeker of credit is living within his means, is progressive, enjoys a good standing and is in an established position. Much tact, however, is required in the handling of individuals; a credit limit is usually established on each account, so that an assistant may pass on orders as they come in from time to time from the various departments. The co-operation of the department managers and bookkeeping and collections departments is very necessary to enable the credit man to properly exercise his function in this respect. A newcomer's antecedents should be investigated very carefully. If possible, the reason for a newcomer having changed from his previous location should always be determined, as this will give a clue as to some of the general characteristics of the applicant. A man who moves around the country without any definite purpose in view, leaving unpaid bills stringing along behind him wherever he goes, is, of course, not entitled to credit and an investigation of antecedents can and usually will disclose these facts.

To watch credits and collect money is not sufficient. A credit man can actually become an important adjunct of the selling organization by increasing sales—without any expense he can be a large factor in getting repeat orders. A credit man can make more customers pay up, and then quit purchasing, more surely than any other man in the organization; but systematic, tactful, diplomatic letters of the proper spirit will develop into good salesmen and probable order getters and good collectors as well.

It is profitable for a credit man and for his house to assist in building up and expanding the business of customers by advice and help. If a customer of yours gets behind in his payments an analysis of the reason for this condition can be made by a study of the financial statement of the customer. If the customer is overstocked, suggestions can be made for moving the stock by proper sales campaigns; if too much money is outstanding, accounts can be realized on by suggesting to the customer the methods of conducting a collection campaign; if the business has fallen off and expenses are out of proportion to volume, suggestions can be made for cutting expenses. Advice covering whatever may be necessary for your customer to do to put his operations on the right side of the ledger will not only enable that customer to pay his obligation to you, but you will be more than repaid in the future business you will secure from one who has profited by your advice.

It requires an analysis of each particular case to know what suggestions of value can be made to the customer, but if you get the confidence of your debtors so that they are frank with you and will come to you and tell you their troubles, or write them to you, much misunderstanding and difficulty will be avoided, and that harmony and goodfellowship in business will be established that is profitable to both buyer and seller.

If statements are made by seekers of credit that cannot be verified, credit should be refused. If a man makes an unqualified statement that he owns a certain piece of real estate and investigation discloses that it stands in the name of his wife, credit should be refused unless the wife guarantees payment or joins in the obligation with her husband.

Many organizations, particularly the local associations of the National Association of Credit Men, maintain prosecution committees and have a prosecution fund with which to prosecute fraudulent debtors. A credit man should discourage all forms of dishonesty and offer by his own individual effort and by his effort in conjunction with organized committees to make it difficult for commerical crooks to prosper.

The author believes, however, that one of the most effective ways of discouraging dishonesty is not so much in the prosecution of dishonest debtors as in careful investigation of all applicants for credit and the absolute refusal of credit to those whose statements are found to be lacking in truth.

CHAPTER III

SOURCES OF INFORMATION AND FORMS SUGGESTED, TO BE OBTAINED FROM SALESMEN

Where salesmen are employed they should be taught and instructed to send in with each order from a new customer all the information they can concerning the financial standing of the buyer. A salesman can be taught to get the necessary information from a "touchy" individual, by using a little tact and diplomacy, without letting the customer know that he is actually getting the information. Much of it can be obtained in conversation with the customer in a casual way, just as though the salesman was interested in his business. Other information can be obtained by mere observation of the premises, and still additional information can be obtained from a local bank and occasionally from other merchants in the town. Sometimes information can be obtained from salesmen representing other concerns selling to this customer with whom your salesman is acquainted.

When a full and complete report is received from the salesman, it gives the credit man some information to start with and as soon as a substantial part of it is verified, the order can always be passed more quickly than when no information has been given. If no information is sent in with the order, or if the concern from whom the order is received does not enjoy a well-established rating with the mercantile agencies, the credit man is plunged into a sort of fishing expedition.

The following are samples of blanks recommended for Salesman's Credit Reports; the first being a form upon which to report merchants; the second, manufacturers; the third, farmers; the fourth, oil producers; and the fifth, metal mining companies:

MERCHANTS' FORM

SALESMAN'S NEW CUSTOMER REPORT

SMITH, BROWN & CO.

(To be filled out and sent in with each new customer's order)

Name..
(*Be sure Name is correct*)
City............................State......................

Age?..................Habits?..........................
Business?..
Length of time engaged in this business?......................
Banks with?..
Owns store building?......................................
Owns real estate?..
Encumbrances?..
Stock valued at?...
Insurance?...
Supposed net worth?.......................................

Business ability?..
Competition?...
Ever fail?..
Buys from?...
    (Give all names that could be used for reference)

....
To what amount would you recommend credit?................
Remarks:..
....
....

                                    ....
Date....................   Salesman.

Suggestions to assist salesmen in getting the information called for by these reports are very helpful. Analyzing the first report to be sent in by salesmen who take a first order from merchants or dealers, the following suggestions are offered:

Age: It is not always necessary to inquire the prospect's age, and it can be explained to the salesman that if the personality of the buyer indicates he might construe this as a personal question, it will be sufficient for the salesman to estimate or guess at the age of the prospect. It is, however, very desirable for a credit man to have some idea of the age of the debtor, because it is an important factor, as has been previously shown.

Habits: A man's habits are usually ascertainable in the same method that information concerning his business ability can be obtained. It is very important, however, to know the habits of the buyer. It should be stated whether his habits are good or bad and whether he is reputed to pay promptly or otherwise; whether he gives the business close attention or not should also be stated.

Business: This blank space is left for the purpose of filling in the kind of business the prospect is engaged in; that is, whether it is a general merchandise business, shoe business, machinery business, or any other specific kind of business. This information the salesman can readily get.

Length of time engaged in this business: The time the prospect has been engaged in business can be learned without any difficulty, usually in a casual way. Most men are proud to make statements as to the length of time they have been engaged in business and the experience they have had. If, however, the salesman should experience any difficulty in getting this information from the prospect, he can get it from prospect's bank, where he will call for additional information any way.

Banks with: It is usually necessary to find out the name of the prospect's bank by direct question, but every buyer understands he must furnish some reference and make some statements as to his standing, unless he has made a statement to the mercantile agencies, and even then he will not object to giving the name of his bank or such specific information as the salesman may desire. Therefore, no difficulty whatever should be experienced by any salesman in learning the name of prospective customer's bank, though it may take some tact and diplomacy to get some of the other information.

Owns store building: Ordinarily it is not difficult for a shrewd salesman to learn from the buyer whether he rents or owns the store he occupies, and also whether he owns any other real estate, but it is not always easy to learn the amount of the encumbrances, asked for by the next question.

Encumbrances: Usually the buyer's banker knows what the buyer's mortgages amount to, and any other encumbrances that may exist; or if convenient, this can be readily learned from the County Recorder's office. If the particular town where the prospect lives is the County seat, the salesman can get the information by calling on the Recorder. If the bank cannot furnish the amount of encumbrances and the County seat is located elsewhere, the salesman should so state, so that the credit man can write to the County Recorder for the necessary information.

Stock valued at: It is not usually difficult to get the prospect to make a statement of the value of his stock, though it must be remembered that most of the owners are likely to overvalue their stock, and due allowance must be made for depreciation and for obsolete stock, which is usually inventoried at cost and usually claimed to be worth it. Salesman should be taught to show in the remarks column whether the stock is well kept or poorly kept, and whether it is up-to-date or growing obsolete.

Insurance: The amount of insurance can usually be obtained in conversation, or from the bank. Most salesmen will regard this of little consequence, but a credit man will realize that a merchant who is careless enough not to cover himself by insurance is not a desirable risk. That carelessness probably extends to other branches of his business, and a fire loss or casualty loss (if there is a workmen's compensation law in the State) might wipe him out entirely. Salesmen should be carefully cautioned that it is necessary to learn to what extent their new customer is covered by insurance.

Supposed net worth: This information may be gleaned in conversation with the buyer, or it may be necessary to get it from the bank referred to.

Business ability: This question must be answered by expression of opinion, based on personal conversation, observation and what may be learned from local townspeople or other salesmen, or from the local banker.

Competition: The character of competition of a new customer can usually be answered from information obtained in conversation, or by observation, or by local inquiry.

Ever failed? This information is usually obtained in

the same method that information concerning the three questions immediately preceding is obtained.

To what amount would you recommend credit? This is a very important question, and credit men should insist upon salesmen answering this question in some way. It will compel the salesman to exercise more care in answering the other questions on the credit report blank, especially if he knows that he is on record as to his recommendation of credit, and while he realizes that he is not responsible directly in case of loss, he knows that his judgment is liable to be checked up later on if difficulty should be experienced in making collection or if the account should develop into a bad one. He is sure to give you more assistance if he has recommended a line of credit, and he is also sure to realize that it is not a safe proposition to recommend credit if he knows there is a serious question about the buyer being good for the amount.

Buys from: This information should not be difficult to ascertain, as usually the character of the goods will indicate to the salesman where they are bought. In many lines of business the brands of the goods themselves will give the salesman a line on this. If not, conversation with the prospective buyer will bring it out.

Remarks: In this space the salesman can give any general information not covered by the questions provided.

After you get your salesmen trained to use these

blanks, some of them will be so careful in getting the information that you can very largely depend upon it to make shipment of some orders without waiting to verify all the detail as to the financial standing of the customer. It is, of course, always important to verify these statements, but an opening order of reasonable amount can sometimes be passed based on the information accompanying the order furnished by the salesman.

The next blank shown is suggested to be used as a basis for use of the credit man in designing one to suit the special requirements of the institution he represents, in case the sales are largely with manufacturers. The manufacturing field is so broad that it would be impossible to design a blank that would cover all phases of the manufacturing business, but the blank following may be used as a guide in designing a blank that will compel the salesman to furnish such information as the credit man might desire, particularly from small manufacturers who may not be rated by the mercantile agencies or who have not become thoroughly established.

MANUFACTURERS' FORM

SALESMAN'S NEW CUSTOMER REPORT

SMITH, BROWN & CO.

(To be filled out and sent in with each new customer's order)

Name...
  (*Be sure Name is correct*)
City...........................State....................

Age?..................Habits?..........................
  (*If an individual*)
Length of time engaged in this business?......................
  (*If a corporation how long organized*)
Names of principals interested?.............................
....
Do you consider interested parties experienced?................
Character of business?.....................................
Banks with?..
Own or lease plant?......Do you consider the plant modern?....
Does the plant impress you as being in good condition?..........
Amount of insurance?........Estimate value of plant?..........
Amount of encumbrances or bonds outstanding?................
Have the principals other interests?..........................
Is the market local or general?..............................
Are specialties made or standard articles manufactured?..........
Competition?..
Buys from? ....
  (*Give all names that could be used for reference*)
....

28 MERCANTILE CREDITS AND COLLECTIONS

To what amount would you recommend credit?.................
Remarks..
....
....
Date......................   Salesman.

The information required by the salesman to properly fill out the manufacturers' credit report can be gotten in the same way that information concerning merchants is procured. It is deemed unnecessary to draw up any additional suggestions in that respect. Some of the questions, of course, cover an entirely different field than the information necessary from merchants, but each question is sufficiently self-explanatory to indicate the source from which such information can be secured.

FARMERS' FORM

SALESMAN'S NEW CUSTOMER REPORT

SMITH, BROWN & CO.

(To be filled out and sent in with each new customer's order)

Name...
              (*Be sure Name is correct*)
City...........................State....................

Age?..................Habits?...........................
Banks with?..
Number of acres in farm?.......Value per acre?..............
Value of improvements?.........Value of livestock?...........

Encumbrances on land?.......................................
Chattel mortgages on livestock?.............................
Kinds of crops grown?.......................................
Supposed net worth?...
Buys from?..
(*Give all names that could be used for reference*)

To what amount would you recommend credit?.................
Remarks:..
....
....

Date.....................   Salesman.

Analyzing the salesmen's new customer report on Farmers, the following recommendations are offered:

Age: The same suggestions as have been referred to in connection with merchants or dealers blanks apply equally as well to farmers.

Habits: Same suggestions are offered as in connection with the merchants' credit report blanks.

Banks with: Same suggestions are offered as in the case of merchants or dealers.

Number of acres in farm: This is very easy to get, because every farmer takes pride in quoting the number of acres of land he owns. Salesmen should be instructed to state in answer to this question whether the land is owned by the farmer, worked on shares or leased, or this can be covered under the subject of remarks.

Value per acre: The value of the land can be obtained

in conversation with the owner. This gives the owner's estimate of the value. The bank will also furnish a statement of the value of the land, or it can be obtained in the neighborhood, as in most districts land in a particular area has a fairly well-established and known value.

Value of improvements: Unless the salesman obtained some estimate of the value of the improvements from conversation with the prospective buyer, he must use his own judgment as to the value of the improvements on the farm.

Value of livestock: An estimate of the value of the farmer's livestock can be obtained by learning something as to the number of head of various kinds of livestock owned.

Encumbrances on land: The encumbrances may be learned from the prospective buyer, or from the buyer's bank, in the same way that it is suggested this information be gotten under the discussion of the merchants' credit reports.

Chattel mortgages on livestock: Salesman must get this information either from the buyer in conversation, from his banker or from the records.

Kinds of crops grown: This is obtained either from conversation or observation.

Supposed net worth: Same suggestions are offered as in connection with the merchants' credit report blanks.

To what amount would you recommend credit: Same

suggestions are offered as in connection with the merchants' credit report blanks.

Buys from: Suggest that here be given the names of dealers from whom the farmer purchases his implements and supplies, which is usually from a recognized implement house or from the local merchants.

Remarks: This space is provided so that the salesman can fill in anything not covered by the printed questions in the blank.

OIL WELL SUPPLIES

SALESMAN'S NEW CUSTOMER REPORT

SMITH, BROWN & CO.

(To be filled out and sent in with each new customer's order)

Name..
     (*Be sure Name is correct*)
City............................State....................

Age?....................Habits?..........................
   (*If an Individual*)
Length of time engaged in this business?........................
       (*If a corporation how long organized*)
Names of principals interested?................................
....
Banks with?...
Number of acres held?.............Owned or leased?...........
Number of wells producing?......Number of wells drilling?......
Amount of royalty?..
Markets oil through?..

Depth of wells in this district?................................
Average gravity of oil produced?.............................
Estimated value of land owned?..............................
Estimated value of leasehold interests?........................
What are the drilling requirements?...........................
What are the forfeiture conditions in the leases?................
Character and amount of encumbrances?......................
Buys from?..
      (*Give all Names that could be used for reference*)
....
To what amount would you recommend credit?..................
Remarks:..
....
....
Date.....................   Salesman.

Getting reliable information from producers of crude oil presents a little different problem. Frequently the supplies for wells—casings, drilling tools, machinery, etc.—is purchased by a superintendent on the ground, while the executive offices, or principals of the company familiar with the terms of the lease, the amount of royalty, forfeiture conditions, and amount of encumbrances, are elsewhere. Sometimes the material is ordered by a purchasing agent, who is not familiar with these facts. But whatever information the salesman can get from the field superintendent or purchasing agent, or the party placing the order, should be filled out, as it will assist the credit man in completing his investigation.

If the operator is an individual his age should be shown, and habits. If a corporation, it should be stated how long they have been organized and what their habits of pay might be.

Names of principals interested: This can easily be obtained from the superintendent.

Banks with: This can easily be obtained from the superintendent.

All the other information called for can be obtained through the superintendent, except possibly the amount of the royalty, the drilling requirements, the forfeiture conditions in the leases, and the character and amount of encumbrances. Frequently this information can be secured in the field, but if the salesman cannot get that information the superintendent should state the name of the secretary or other executive officer in charge of the main office of the company, so that the credit man may make inquiry on these points by correspondence.

It is very important for a credit man whose firm sells oil well supplies to get the information called for in the report. Mercantile agencies seldom give information of the character sought. Seldom do any of the mercantile agencies show the drilling requirements, forfeiture conditions, marketing arrangements, depth of wells in the district, and gravity of oil produced.

It is not possible to state what percentage of royalty is prohibitive, for in some districts with shallow wells and high gravity oil the cost of production is small, and a higher royalty can be paid in that case than in the case of a concern producing a low gravity oil from deep, expensive wells. Also, the hazard is greater in some fields than in others, and the hazard is always greater in deep wells than in shallow wells. If tools are lost in a deep well the cost of fishing them out is very expensive, and sometimes a well on which thousands of dollars have been spent has been lost by dropping the tools.

It is important to know the marketing arrangement, so that if a debtor gets behind you can get an order on the company through which the product is marketed, or if it is necessary to institute legal proceedings the purchaser of the oil may be garnisheed. Of course, if the market is general and the oil is sold to the general public the case is different, but most producers of crude oil market their oil through some agency and not directly to the public.

The drilling requirements are also important to know. If the lease compels the subject of inquiry to drill a certain number of wells per year, regardless of the market price of oil, the corporation may be embarrassed by the expensive drilling at a time when the oil must be sold below the cost of production. A fair lease should provide that when oil goes below a certain specified price per barrel, the drilling requirements are suspended until the market recovers.

SOURCES OF INFORMATION AND FORMS

Many losses are sustained by unfair forfeiture conditions in the lease. Most leases provide that on failure to pay the royalty, failure to drill wells, and technical abandonment of the property, or for other reasons amounting to a forfeiture, all improvements shall forthwith revert to the lessor. This is not equitable and such an agreement may not be upheld by the courts, but it is very embarrassing to a credit man to find that after he caused the property to be attached that the lessor presents an affidavit claiming the ownership of the improvements, thereby releasing the attachment, unless the seller furnishes a bond, which may involve him in an action for damages. Where the forfeiture clause is unreasonable, independent security should be obtained, usually the written guarantee of responsible interested parties.

All the other questions in the credit report are self-explanatory.

The next report is a suggestion for a credit blank to be used by concerns selling to the metal mining industry. It does not particularly cover coal mining operations, but most coal mining companies are pretty well established and rated; if not, the following blank gives an idea of the form in which information can be sought, with such changes as apply to coal mines; such as, the kind of coal mined, market, depth, whether it is a prospective mine or a producing mine. In fact, it is only on prospective mines that credit information is necessary as producing coal mines enjoy a complete rating.

The questions shown are self-explanatory, and most of them can be answered from information obtained from the superintendent or officer placing the order.

Promoters of prospects understand that deals with mining companies are cash, or that the obligation must be well secured, and even though there has been some development on the mine it is usually very hazardous to extend a line of credit to mining companies unless the company furnishes security or a satisfactory written guarantee.

MINING DEPARTMENT

SALESMAN'S NEW CUSTOMER REPORT

SMITH, BROWN & CO.

(*To be filled out and sent in with each new customer's order*)

Name...
  (*Be sure Name is correct*)
City............................State......................

Age?................Habits?...........................
  (*If an individual*)
Length of time engaged in this business?...................
  (*If a corporation how long organized*)
Names of principals interested?...........................
....
Banks with?..
Is the mine a prospect or has it an established production?.......
Number of men employed?..................................

Are claims held on location or patented?......................
Distance from railroad?.....Distance from nearest smelter?......
Character of ore mined?.......Depth of main shaft?...........
What endorsements or other security offered?...................
What are the encumbrances?................................
Is it a close corporation or is the stock scattered?...............
Is the mine well equipped?...................................
What is the value of the improvements?.......................
Buys from?...
(*Give all names that could be used for reference*)
....
To what amount would you recommend credit?................
Remarks:..
....
....
Date.................... Salesman.

No attempt will be made to outline the form of credit blank to be used where merchandise is sold at retail to the general buying public, for the reason that there are so many different classifications of retail business that no general form would be suitable for the purpose. Furthermore, some credit men prefer to have a signed application for credit executed by the individual, and also it makes a difference whether the purchases are largely made by the wife of the customer to whom the goods are charged.

It is necessary, however, to get the full name of the purchaser, and if the purchases are made by the wife, the full name of the husband, the character, residence, address, the occupation of the husband, the length of time employed by the firm he is then connected with, the length of time applicant has resided in the city, and if a newcomer where they came from. The name of a bank should be secured, and also provision made to ascertain if property is owned, where the business being transacted will permit. Where signed applications are required, it is desirable to include in the questions whether the applicant owns or rents his home, and also whether his life is insured. A married man with a family who has been thoughtful enough to provide life insurance is usually a more steady sort of an individual than one who is not so thoughtful. It is, of course, important to get the names of other local merchants with whom credit has been established, but local utilities should not be accepted as references, because almost every one pays these bills, knowing the supply of gas, water and electric light will be shut off if they do not.

It is well to distinguish between an established individual and one who is not so. By established is meant one who has followed certain lines of business and has shown progress, rather than one who has embarked in a new character of employment every little while, or who has changed his position frequently, even in the same line of business.

CREDIT DEPARTMENT

SMITH, BROWN & CO.

Chicago, Ill., ..., 19 .

....
....
....

Gentlemen:—

Please give us below in confidence information concerning the financial responsibility, habits of pay, business ability and character of...
Who has (has not) referred to you.

We will treat the information as confidential and accept same without responsibility to you, and thank you in advance for your courtesy.

We will be pleased to reciprocate when opportunity offers.

Yours truly,
SMITH, BROWN & CO.
By............................

Amount involved?..
Occupation or Business?....................................
Pays promptly?..
Estimated net worth?......................................
Are sight drafts frequently drawn?........................
Are they paid or dishonored?..............................
Other information?..
....
....
....

(Signature.)

It is usually desirable to send bank inquiries to several banks in the same town and if the customer has not referred to any particular bank, it may be necessary to send blanks to all the banks in the town. Many banks will not give you all the information sought, but will simply say, "Good for the amount" or "We consider good." These are rather indefinite statements, but are sometimes helpful in connection with other information obtained from other sources.

The following blank is suitable to obtain information from other merchants by mail:

CREDIT DEPARTMENT

SMITH, BROWN & CO.

Chicago, Ill.,............, 19 .

....
....
....

Gentlemen:

We have an order from, and desire information concerning the financial responsibility, habits of pay, business ability, and character of..

Will you kindly advise us your experience? We thank you in advance for your courtesy, and will be pleased to reciprocate when opportunity offers.

Yours truly,
SMITH, BROWN & CO.
By............................

Amount involved..
Occupation or Business?.....................................
How long sold?..

Highest credit within the last year?............................
Pays?...
Other information?..
....
....
(Signature.)

The best indication as to whether a customer pays promptly or not is the information obtained from the concerns with which he deals. No matter what his bank account may show, or the amount of stock he carries, or how much business he does, if he is not paying other merchants satisfactorily, he is not likely to pay you on a satisfactory basis. An experienced credit man relies on information obtained from this source to a very great extent. In cities where credit men are organized as a branch of the National Association of Credit Men, or in other communities where independent credit organizations exist, this information is usually obtained over the telephone from fellow members. When it is necessary to get the information from out of town sources, it may be obtained either by a blank or by letter. A blank is usually sufficient, but if the case is an unusual one, or the order requires immediate attention, or there are other factors that make it appear desirable to use a letter, a special letter of inquiry should be sent. It should be your policy to cooperate, as pointed out in a succeeding chapter, with these merchants, banks, and with the salesmen in getting the information as well as expecting to receive it.

The preceding sources of information, in addition to oral investigations and interviews made by the credit man, have no reference, of course, to the sources most generally employed—that of obtaining reports from commerical agencies. These reports are obtained by filling out a subscriber's ticket and forwarding it to the mercantile agency, who usually have on file statements from active or established institutions. If they do not have such reports, they get one from their correspondent or through their traveling reporters, or by mail direct from the subject of the inquiry. The information from other sources, however, will tend to check up the report you get from the mercantile agency. The proper analysis of these reports will be explained in a succeeding chapter.

If the character of the business is such that it is desirable to get a report from an attorney, a number of institutions have lists of approved attorneys who will furnish reports for a reasonable sum each, and some lawyers will furnish general information without charge to clients who they may have reason to believe will favor them with legal business at some later date. If a blank is used to send to an attorney by the seller himself, it should be in the general form as the blank sent to banks, with such added information concerning suits, judgments, property, mortgages, etc., as may be wanted.

However, attorneys as a class are not very good about filling out a blank and returning it, and the best results can usually be obtained from a lawyer by writing him a letter. The practice of sending blanks to attorneys upon which to get information is not recommended.

CHAPTER V

METHOD OF COMPILING INFORMATION AND FINAL DISPOSITION OF ORDERS

The most satisfactory way of filing credit information is in a folder, perferably of the vertical type. In that folder should be filed the report from the salesman, the report from the mercantile agency, the reports from banks, from other merchants, and the financial statements made on your own blank by the customer, and information from any other source. If a credit man gets information over the telephone, it is well to make a memorandum of it right after the conversation, usually by dictating the essence of the information to the stenographer in the form of a memorandum for the files, and this information should be filed in the credit folder. All subsequent information concerning the financial standing of that particular customer should be filed in this folder, and all reports should be bradded together, with the first information received on the bottom and the latest information received on the top. In this way automatically your credit folder is kept in date order, with the latest information striking the eye first.

It is recommended that a credit limit be written in on the report most relied upon by the credit man, and this credit limit should be transferred to a card by some stenographer or clerk in the office. The information should be kept up to date, and the credit limits revised as occasion may require. The card fixing the credit limit should be promptly sent in to the bookkeeping department, so that the credit limit may be immediately transferred to the ledger and the bookkeeper should initial the credit limit card showing that same has been noted on the customer's ledger account. A cipher or code should be used on the ledger, denoting the credit limit, to prevent the customer from seeing the limit on his account if he should call to settle and the ledger used before him for the purpose of settlement. After the credit limit has been fixed, an assistant in the office of the credit man can pass on credits, and there is a double check on seeing that the customers do not exceed the limit fixed, not only by the credit man or his assistants watching the limit cards in the card system but by the bookkeepers as well.

It is the duty of the bookkeeper to call the credit department's attention to the fact that the sum total owing on an account has practically reached, or has exceeded, the credit limit, when that condition occurs.

In some sections of the country a daily notification sheet is issued by either the mercantile agencies or some local organization, and frequently in large communities credit men subscribe to some of the daily law journals, or record sheets, showing everything that is recorded in that County on the day previous. If information affecting any of your customers is received from any of these sources, or if you receive one of the tissue sheet notifications from the mercantile agencies of any change in a customer's affairs, it should all be filed in the credit folder, and a change in credit limit made at the time, if any change is necessary due to the receipt of this information. It is essential to keep the credit folders up to date, and it is a good practice to get reports and revise your credit information even on some of the older customers. There are changes occurring in all their affairs, and merely because a customer has been a throughly satisfactory customer for several years is not always proof that he will always be prosperous and entitled to the limit you have fixed on his account.

If credit is not extended and an initial order is declined, that fact should be noted on the report most strongly relied upon by the credit man, and a card should be made out showing there is a report on file on the subject of the inquiry but that credit was declined. In this case, of course, it is unnecessary to send the card to the bookkeeper to be noted on the ledger. Later on, however, this particular party may again seek credit, and having since then prospered may be entitled to it, in which case the old card is taken out and a new one placing a limit thereon is substituted, and the first card can be filed in the credit folder.

Some credit men prefer to endorse on the outside of

the credit folder a memorandum of each report received, and also the unfilled orders on hand approved but not yet shipped. As to whether or not this is necessary largely depends upon the individual opinion of the credit man interested. If the credit data, however, is properly bradded together and filed in the credit folder it is not necessary to endorse a list of the reports on the outside, that being merely an added convenience only in case it is thought desirable.

When an order from a new customer is accepted a letter of acceptance should be written to the customer, expressing thanks in appropriate terms and making such statements as the character of the business might require. As previously stated, this practice tends to put the credit department in closer touch with the customer when business relations are first commenced. First impressions are usually lasting, and it is good business for any credit man to have a customer form a good impression of him at first. It may be very helpful later, when conditions have changed the financial affairs of the customer. It is also recommended that a carbon copy of the letter of acceptance be sent to the salesman who secured the order. This establishes a closer relation with the salesman and tends for better co-operation.

The next thing to do is to approve the order, and immediately after it is approved it should be placed with the proper department—either the shipping department or order department—for prompt attention. Some concerns have established a policy so broad that the credit department is required to temporarily approve an order, so that all its component parts may be gotten together ready for shipment in case it is accepted. In that case, a rubber stamp should be placed on the order, instructing the shipping department to get final approval of the credit department before the shipment is made. The final approval should be written boldly across the rubber stamp requiring such final approval. Of course, if the order is declined there is some little expense putting the material back in stock, but as the bulk of the orders received are accepted this expense is comparatively small compared with the added business gained by giving customers prompt service.

After having exhausted every effort to obtain a remittance or security, or in any other manner put the order into acceptable shape, and the credit man finds he positively must decline the order, circumstances should determine as to what sort of a communication should be addressed to the customer, but the refusal to fill the order should be so couched that the "sting" has been removed from it and so that it will not create a spirit of resentment in the mind of the customer when he reads it. It is not always possible to do this, but great care should be exercised in the phraseology of a letter notifying the customer that his order cannot be accepted. This same customer may recoup his financial condition later and become a desirable risk, and if he has become embittered by the fact that credit was refused him, your sales organization will be at a serious disadvantage in attempting to sell him and may be wholly unable to ever get him on your list as a customer even when it is known that he is in first-class financial condition. Copies of letters declining orders should always be sent to the salesman so that he is fully informed of the final action taken by the house, in disposing of the order.

A careful record should be kept of all orders that are declined, either in your credit folders or on your card system, if a card system is used—especially if a card system defining credit limitations is in operation. And if orders are received from the same customer to whom credit has been refused before, if a reasonable time has elasped since the last order was turned down, it is advisable to look up the customer's standing again, as it may have improved, and a careful investigation of the order then under consideration might indicate that credit might be safely extended at that time. In the succeeding chapter attention will be called to the necessity of using diplomacy in declining orders.

CHAPTER VI

CO-OPERATION AND DIPLOMACY

It requires tact, skill and diplomacy to get the necessary co-operation from salesmen and customers. The idea that the credit department and sales department are natural born enemies is a mistaken one, and credit men should remember that co-operation means something mutual. Salesmen are naturally enthusiastic, otherwise they would not be good salesmen, and it is but natural that their spirit is dampened when an order is rejected, especially if they have difficulty in obtaining it by reason of the competition encountered, or because the customer was hard to convince and sell. A long step in the right direction is to tell a salesman why an order has been rejected, and not merely state that it was rejected because the customer's credit was no good. No intelligent credit man will accept an order of any consequence and rely entirely upon the salesman's statement, "This man's credit is O K, please rush." An intelligent salesman feels just as bad when he learns that an order has been declined without any other statement being given him than that the customer's credit was unsatisfactory. It may not be necessary to give the salesman much detail information, but a specific reason for declining the order should be given, by stating that the customer was overexpanded, or that he was owing too much money long past due, or any other specific reason that prompts a credit man to reject the order. Experience has shown that the business of a house prospers most when the sales department and the credit department are working in harmony, for it is teamwork that counts and not internal organization strife.

It has already been stated that one of the functions of a credit man is to furnish the salesman with a list of good credit risks in the territory that the salesman is about to visit. Much good can also be accomplished by furnishing the salesman with a pocket edition of either Dun's or Bradstreet's rating books. Mercantile agencies furnish subscribers with these books for a small amount. This gives the salesman some idea of the credit rating of the customers in his territory. Some credit men even go so far as to notify the salesman that a credit limit has been placed on an account, and some state the amount of such limit, but each credit man must determine the advisability of such a policy, depending upon the circumstances.

When a customer's account is past due, it is desirable to send the salesman a copy of all correspondence bearing on collection. Frequently the salesman can help you collect an account if he is fully informed as to its status. The salesman can also assist you in adjusting disputes or controversies, and he will be more inclined to render this friendly assistance if he feels that you are working with him and for him and not against him.

All salesmen should be required to send in a credit report on new customers, and salesmen should be furnished with printed blanks and written instructions as to what is expected of them in this report.

Credit men should bear in mind that credit accounts do not occur until a salesman has first made a sale; and salesmen should be taught the theory that a sale is not a sale until the goods are paid for and the money is in the bank. Bad debts represent not only the value of the merchandise which has been lost, but represent continual losses in time expended by the salesman, credit department and collection department, and practically by every employee in the house. A salesman who knowingly accepts an order, or who could by the use of diligence ascertain that there is danger of the goods not being paid for, is just as culpable as a cashier who knowingly accepts counterfeit money. The loss represented by a sale that develops into a bad debt is measured not only by the loss of the goods and profit thereon, but all the selling and overhead expense are an additional loss.

All salesmen do not understand this situation, because they have given it little thought, or because they have had no training or experience. It is hard for them to believe that a congenial customer who is glad to see them and places a nice order, and who has every appearance of being prosperous, can possibly be a poor risk. Salesmen are prone to confuse inability to pay with dishonesty, and they resent the rejection of an order as an imputation that their good-fellow customer is not an honorable man.

A credit man can, however, by co-operating with a salesman and keeping him informed by copies of correspondence with delinquent customers in his territory, and by requiring information from salesmen, and training them to analyze a new customer through the use of the blanks shown previously herein, remove the barrier that often exists between the credit department and the sales department.

It is also desirable to have the co-operation of the customers themselves. This can be accomplished in several different ways. It is very effective to start a customer off right; to have a letter of thanks written through the credit department when the account is opened. A credit man does not lose any of his effective hold on a customer by this method, but he does instill a feeling of good will at the very inception of doing business. First impressions are lasting, and if the customer's first conception of the credit department of the house is good, it goes a long way towards keeping that feeling alive and active. Sometimes as part of the sales campaign, a postcript on the credit department or collection letters to the effect that prices on a certain article are likely to go up, not only brings in business, but makes the customer feel closer to the credit man. A friendly letter to a customer who seems to be overstocked, suggesting that some campaign should be inaugurated to turn this stock into liquid capital is valuable. Letters like this should not be sent in a spirit of criticism, but in a spirit of helpfulness and in a spirit which is meant to be of assistance, and not of a critical character. Likewise, if a large part of the customer's assets is invested in slow-moving accounts, helpful suggestions as to the method of conducting a collection campaign are very beneficial. It is a notable fact that credit men who have succeeded to the greatest extent in holding the good will of their customers, get their money first, and also know first of any pending disturbance in the customer's affairs, and are enabled to get security, while other less fortunate concerns whose credit men have not cultivated the proper co-operation of the customer are left to face a loss. When this friendly spirit has been highly developed, customers will come to a credit man with their troubles for assistance and advice, and receive good, sound advice from an experienced business man, which engenders in them lasting faith, and which helps your business relations with them from every angle.

Wherever possible it is also desirable for credit men to co-operate with banks. While a bank is usually under obligation to its customers to give information concerning its depositors who refer to them, the information is often more complete if the credit department is known to the bank in an agreeable way. Banks usually give out more information than they seek, and in sending an inquiry to a bank by mail a much better feeling is established if a stamped and addressed return envelope accompanies the inquiry. Inquiry blanks sent to financial institutions should also state that the favor will be gladly reciprocated whenever opportunity offers, so that if this bank later requires some information on this customer from a commercial standpoint, the bank will understand that you will furnish them as readily with information as they have furnished it to you.

This same theory applies to other merchants from whom you seek information. It is a good thing for business interests that the old feeling of prejudice that information regarding a customer was strictly confidential and should not be given to a competitive house has disappeared. Very few concerns are now so narrow that they will undertake to get information for the benefit of their sales department through their credit department. If this practice is followed your source of information will soon be cut off, but if the information concerning the customer's account is interchanged openly, freely, and in a broadminded way, and not used for the purpose of taking trade from your informant, you not only have a valuable source of information, but your danger of losses is less. There is a difference of opinion as to whether or not ledger information should be exchanged between credit men of competitive houses, but the feeling on this broadminded practice, previously regarded with considerable prejudice, has now practically disappeared, the exceptions to the rule being very rare.

In cities where credit men are organized into a local credit association, ledger information is usually gathered together by this association and the total amount of a customer's obligations are shown, together with the total amount past due, and various expressions of opinion concerning the debtor.

This same spirit of co-operation should be exhibited when creditors' meetings are called, for it is useless for one unsecured creditor to attempt to gain an advantage over the other, and it is usually better for secured creditors to grant an extension, to make it easier for the unsecured creditors to realize on their claims, so long as the rights of the secured creditors are not violated or prejudiced, nor their security lessened or impaired. At the next creditors' meeting you may find yourself with an unsecured claim, and you may be urging an extension on behalf of the debtor to enable him to work out his affairs and pay his debts from secured creditors who were unsecured at the last meeting of some other important debtor.

In this connection it is proper to say that extensions

should only be granted for some consideration, and it is a very good policy to require full information from a customer seeking an extension, and the following blank is a great help in obtaining necessary facts and tends to discourage the promiscuous requests for additional time. The blanks should be in regular printed form, and one should be sent to each seeker of an extension with a letter asking the customer to fill it out, stating the application will be carefully considered as soon as received. It is distasteful to fill out a blank and many customers will pay rather than go through all this formality, especially if they fear they cannot show some adequate reason for not paying.

APPLICATION FOR EXTENSION OF TIME OF PAYMENT

........................(Place)
....................19   (Date)

JNO DOE & Co.,

....
....

Gentlemen:

........hereby apply to you for an extension of time within
(*I or We*)
which to pay........obligation to you, amounting to............
 (*My or Our*)
........................dollars ($............) due..........
19...
........request that the time of payment of aforesaid obligation
(*I or We*)
be extended by you to.................19.., and as a considera-

tion therefor........will, if said extension is granted by you, pay
    (*I or We*)
.......................dollars ($........) on..............
191., in part payment, and furnish you with the following security, to cover the balance, to wit:
....
....
....

The reason ....can not pay the obligation at maturity is
    (*I or We*)
....
....

It is understood by........that no agreement on your part to
    (*Me or Us*)
extend the time of payment shall be binding on you until you have determined that the aforesaid security above tendered is satisfactory to you.

                    Very truly yours,
                    ....
                    ....

One of the most perplexing problems a credit man encounters is the problem of declining an order. In the first place, there is a desire to fill the order if possible after it has once been received, and sometimes it is difficult to come to a decision as to whether or not the order should actually be declined. Even though all the information on the subject of inquiry has been verified, the statement of the prospective customer's assets and liabilities and general credit standing sometimes presents a complex situation. A slight turn in the customer's affairs might enable him to take care of his obligations promptly, if that slight turn is favorable, and on the other hand a slightly unfavorable turn may seriously embarrass him, if his affairs are seemingly at the turning point.

It should be remembered that most seekers of credit resent the inference that they are not responsible. Due to their own lack of analysis, sometimes, they actually believe that they are amply responsible. Their intentions are good, but they do not realize their own pending danger. If you have refused to fill an order at a time when their condition does not warrant your extending them credit, they may later recoup themselves and be in good credit standing, and then when your salesman or the house solicits their business they will promptly state what they think of your credit man. Some debtors even become bitter and go out of their way to influence others not to buy from you if you have questioned their credit.

It is not always possible to decline an order and still hold the good will of the debtor, but it is essential to hold his good will wherever possible. Care should therefore be exercised to see that letters declining an order are not abrupt. Your letter should be in an easy, flowing style, and all the rough edges should be trimmed off. It is not advisable to make the plain statement that information on the prospect's financial standing is not satisfactory, but the credit man's letter should express thanks for the business. Then the power of suggestion should be used by stating that pending the usual investigations, which might cause some delay, your suggestion would be that the buyer take advantage of the cash discount and get prompt shipment. If he knows that his credit is somewhat questionable, he will respond promptly, just to show you that he can pay, and he is also prompted by the thought that by prompt payment he will actually establish his credit with the house. Then the salesman can be told to cease soliciting business from that particular customer, so that you will not have to decline his orders. It is better not to take an order at all than to take it and then decline it. This is especially so if either the salesman or credit man know in advance that the order would have to be rejected even if it was taken. That is why it is desirable for the credit and sales department to co-operate. The particular order that you are compelled to decline probably would not have been taken if you had given the salesman a list of good merchants in a town instead of leaving it to the salesman to solicit business wherever he thought it was possible. The same order might have been taken from a good credit risk as well as from a poor one with the same amount of energy and money expended, and there would be more pep and enthusiasm left in the salesman, as declining an order is always bound to dampen his spirits. Many doubtful orders can be converted into good ones and the unpleasantness of having actually to decline the order or of having a "sorehead" on your list can be avoided.

It is also essential to keep the good will of your salesmen, even though you are frequently compelled to decline orders. Some salesmen seem to have the unhappy faculty of taking a lot of business from poor credit risks. In many instances this is due to lack of proper instructions and advice from the credit man and due to the lack of business training the salesman has had. For even though a credit man may have been thoughtless, or overlooked instructing or advising a salesman, some of them naturally have better judgment than others and the ones with the poor judgment turn in the most orders from the poorest credit risks. This is usually the experience of a new salesman. He starts out like a new broom with the intention of making a clean sweep of the whole territory and takes every order in sight. He thinks he is doing a land office business in garnering in a lot of orders that the better trained salesman of your organization would not have taken. On his first trip or two, he bites at all the leftovers, and this is particularly true if he has been started out without proper guidance. At the end of the trip his superior may remark on the small amount of business he has turned in, and his answer usually is that he obtained plenty of business but the credit man, with all his wisdom, took delight in turning his orders down.

But even after a salesman has been throughly coached and throughly advised and instructed as to what is expected of him, and even after he has been furnished with a list of desirable credit risks in the community, some orders will creep in that must be declined. Maybe since the rating of the debtor was made up, his affairs have taken a turn for the worse and at the time the order is received by the house it is not accepted. In some lines of business it is not always possible to furnish the salesmen with a list of good credit risks. If business is not transacted through merchants or dealers, the class of buying public is usually unknown to the credit man. In that case, however, compelling the salesman to use the Salesmen's Credit Blank will be very helpful in retaining his good will, as then he is bound to be careful and gain experience enough to see whether or not his customer stands well. The salesman should always be told the reason why the order has been refused, so he will understand that the reason is a good one. It is a very good practice, if conditions of the business permit, for the credit man to go on the territory once in a while, not only to analyze conditions first hand, but to have the opportunity of being with the salesman when he closes an order, so that the method of going about the getting of credit information can be observed by the salesman in the transaction, each move being directed by the credit man himself. If you both understand each other, the salesman will not feel that you are going to kill his prospect before he gets a chance to sell him.

It is not necessary to cater to the salesman, as you can still command his respect, and, if necessary, be strict in credit matters, and yet, withal, have him feel that you are co-operating with him, and when that feeling is instilled you will keep his good will even though your duty compels you to decline orders received from him that he may in the first place have thought were gilt-edged.

CHAPTER VII

CONVERTING DOUBTFUL ORDERS INTO GOOD ONES AND THE USE OF GUARANTEES

Much resourcefulness is required in dealing with doubtful orders. In the shape they are received it may not be possible to fill them without risk of incurring loss. In a few institutions the demand for product manufactured and sold is so great the credit man may be independent, and even drastic; he may insist on having the cash in advance, knowing that he cannot possibly be criticised for declining sales, because the demand is so active that the same goods can be readily sold to some well-rated concern. This is usually a short-sighted policy, however, because there are very few institutions who will always be oversold; the day may come when their production is greater than the A-1 rated concerns will absorb, and most sellers find competition such that they cannot be so independent, except only in abnormal times. The cost of getting the business has already been expended. For this reason, particularly, it is desirable to try and convert a doubtful order into one that is acceptable. Many orders which cannot be approved in the shape in which they are received can be so converted. One method is by the use of suggestion; a carefully worded diplomatic letter, requiring but little more time than a mere formal letter notifying the customer the order cannot be approved, will often result in saving the business, by causing the customer to remit the amount of the order after deducting the cash discount.

It is of advantage to the credit man to know how badly the goods are required by the buyer, and how soon he could get them elsewhere if the order was declined; for this information will enable him to determine whether it is wise to suggest remitting, less cash discount; remitting to avoid delay in looking up the customer's standing; or whether his suggestion should be in the form of furnishing security.

The following form of letter has been used quite frequently by the author with gratifying results. It can be changed to suit the individual diction of the credit man, or can be rearranged to suit different circumstances, but the thought conveyed is the main element in producing the desired effect on your customer.

Chicago,................, 19...

U. S. CONSUMERS CO.,
   Chicago, Ill.
Dear Sirs:—

   Through our salesman, Mr. Brown, we have been favored with your valued order, amounting to $........, which is having our attention, and for which kindly accept our thanks.

From authorities usually consulted in such matters we seem to be unable to get sufficient information to approve the order promptly, and, therefore, rather than delay shipment, we take the liberty of suggesting that you kindly remit the amount, $........, on which you are entitled to a cash discount of $........, which will avoid any further unfortunate delay.

We thank you in advance for complying with this suggestion, and know you will realize it is made in order that we may give you prompt service.

Yours truly,

Please observe that while this letter is not too long to be burdensome the "sting" is pretty well removed. In starting to read the letter your customer's attention is drawn to the fact that his order is having attention and he is pleased to have your thanks for the business. If you allow cash discounts in your business, the suggestion that he remit and take the cash discount is usually accepted, unless the amount involved is beyond your customer's reach. Furthermore, he is glad to know that you have taken the matter up with him promptly so as not to delay his order, and, lastly, he is impressed by the fact that his first order gets prompt attention and that you are trying to give him prompt service even before he has established his credit. It is very rarely that a customer will resent this form of letter, the only exception being temperamental and over-expanded individuals or those who are involved or living beyond their means.

If your analysis of the situation indicates that it

might be unwise to ask for a remittance, a suggestion can be made that security be furnished, though it is difficult to outline any method or plan by which security of this character can be obtained by mail. The letter requesting such security must necessarily be prompted and phrased according to existing circumstances and conditions, which are different in almost every case. In arranging a large line of credit, however, it is frequently desirable to take some satisfactory real estate or chattel mortgage security if there is any doubt about the financial standing of the buyer. In large matters of this kind usually a credit man does not undertake to obtain the security by mail, but either goes in person to the customer or sends a representative from his department, or if the salesman has been sufficiently trained he can be instructed as to how to approach the buyer and arrange for security.

Frequently, however, corporations, especially speculative corporations having but a limited amount of assets (such as undeveloped mines and oil companies), are backed by men whose individual standing is satisfactory. In this case it is usually possible to convert a doubtful order from such speculative concerns into a good one by obtaining the personal guarantee of responsible individuals interested in the venture. It is true that men of standing hesitate to accept personal liability in corporate matters, but if the matter is presented to them in the proper light very frequently such guarantees can be arranged. One very successful argument is: "How can you expect us to take the risk if you, who are in control of the corporation's affairs are unwilling to take the risk?" And it is a fact if a responsible individual has control of the destiny of a corporation and is unwilling to lend that corporation strength, after assuring the seller that bills will be promptly paid as long as he is connected with it, it is no fit subject for a credit man to take a chance on.

Frequently responsible relatives will guarantee obligations of an individual, and even the landowner will guarantee the obligation of some lessee who is improving his property. It is really necessary to know just what personal relationships exist in order to know who to approach for a guarantee or who should be suggested as a guarantor to the buyer.

As to the use of a sufficient guarantee covering a new account, the following form has been recommended by the National Association of Credit Men.

GUARANTEE OF PAYMENT TO............

........................19...

U. S. CONSUMERS Co.,
  Chicago, Ill.
Dear Sirs:—

  Please sell and deliver to...................................
                        (*Name of party getting the merchandise*)
on your usual credit terms, such goods, wares and merchandise as
....
            (*Name of party getting the merchandise*)

from time to time may select, and in consideration thereof I or we hereby guarantee and hold myself or ourselves personally responsible severally and jointly for the payment at maturity of the purchase price of all such goods, wares and merchandise so sold and delivered, whether evidenced by open account or note. I or we hereby waive notice of acceptance thereof, amount of sales, dates of shipment or delivery, and notice of default in payment. I or we further waive the requirement of legal proceedings against the said purchaser.

This is intended to be a continuing guarantee, applying to all sales made by you to..
(*Name of party getting the merchandise*)
from this date until the same is revoked by me or us in writing.

WITNESS my hand and seal this........day of........19...
....
....
....

It is well to call attention to the fact that in most states the courts will hold that a guarantee in writing promising to make good the default of another is valid only when there has been a sufficient consideration. Of course, if the guarantee is given before the goods are shipped, it follows that the consideration was ample, in that the principal obtained credit and this is always ample consideration. If the guarantee in writing is taken after a debt has been incurred there is a question as to its validity in many states unless the consideration was sufficient, and a sufficient consideration usually is an agreement to extend the obligation, or to forbear to sue, or by extending additional credit, making that a part of the consideration.

It is often the tendency of a guarantor, feeling that he has had no direct benefit from the transaction, to seek to evade payment when calamity befalls his principal. Therefore, in opening up a new account on which credit is extended by reason of your faith in the guarantor the foregoing form of protection should be used.

The following guarantee was held to be insufficient:

"In regard to A's account, will say that you need not worry about this. It may be possible that I will take the stock and close it out for him. He is not insolvent but has simply got overstocked and will be a little slow in paying up, but I will see that you are paid."

In the absence of legal advice, under the circumstances existing in this particular case, any reasonable man would consider that the guarantor was liable; for in this particular case both the principal and the guarantor were ordering goods concurrently on the same venture and at times the principal paid and at other times the guarantor paid, but there was no guarantee of payment taken when the account was opened. However, when the principal became lax in payment the guarantor sent in a letter in the above phraseology, in the belief that the creditor would not further press the obligation as the guarantor was amply responsible. The principal filed a petition in bankruptcy. It was discovered that the guarantor was his largest creditor, and the credit man was advised that it was doubtful if he could recover, as he had not entered into any agreement to forbear to sue, nor did he agree to extend the time of payment, so that there was no definite consideration for the guarantee. The credit man received a letter, accepted it in good faith and relied upon it.

These facts are stated so that a credit man will realize the importance of seeing that there is ample consideration for the acceptance of a guarantee not only when an account is opened (and this is usually always sufficient in that credit is extended to the principal), but also to see that the consideration for the acceptance of a guarantee on an obligation already owing is sufficient, and it is recommended that a promissory note with a definite date of maturity be accepted in such cases, with the guarantor as endorser. This procedure avoids any question of consideration. Where it is not possible to get a note from the debtor with the guarantor's endorsement, the following form of guarantee may be safely used:

GUARANTEE OF PAYMENT OF ACCOUNT OWING TO....

........................19..

JOHN DOE & Co.,
....

Gentlemen:

In consideration that...................., a corporation duly organized and existing under the laws of the State of............, will extend the time of payment of....................Dollars,

now due it from..to the
............day of...................., A. D. 19... I or we, severally and jointly, hereby guarantee the payment of said sum on said last mentioned date by.................................
without requiring any demand or notice of default, and I or we agree that any extension may be granted or additional security taken, or additional security taken surrendered, at any time without notice or affecting my or our liability hereunder. My or our liability, however, is limited to....................................Dollars, together with interest at the legal rate per annum until paid, with all costs, attorneys' fees and expenses that shall arise from enforcing collection of said account.

WITNESS my or our signature..and seal.. this..............
day of...................., A. D. 19...

........................(SEAL)
........................(SEAL)
........................(SEAL)

The co-operation of the salesman is a great help in dealing with orders of this kind; and endeavoring to put an order into acceptable shape stimulates him to work closely with the credit department. Send the salesman a copy of the letter to his new customer. He may be able to give valuable suggestions to assist in handling the matter. And he will be more deeply impressed with the necessity of furnishing full information on new customers.

Efforts to convert doubtful orders into good ones are profitable and a large volume of business can be saved during the course of a year.

CHAPTER VIII

HOW TO READ A FINANCIAL STATEMENT

It is impossible to lay down any specific rule as to how a financial statement should be analyzed, as diversified classes of business require different financial operations, so that only general statements may be made as to how to analyze such statements. The analysis of a statement of an individual must necessarily differ from that which would be applied to a corporation.

In the case of an individual, his age should be carefully considered; for instance, a man 35 or 40 years old would naturally have better business judgment than a young man 21 years old; a man 40 years old may have had 15 years' experience in his particular business, and if experienced in the line then engaged in would be a better credit risk than a young man 21 years old who might have more capital but less experience and less mature judgment.

In the case of a corporation, the experience and age of the officers, directors, or those managing the business is an important factor to the same extent; and the age of the corporation itself is important; for instance, a corporation just organized, having to face all the established competition, presents some uncertainty to the credit man as against an old-established corporation who have already demonstrated their success.

One of the next things to do is to segregate the quick assets and the quick liabilities. Quick assets usually consist of cash, good accounts and notes receivable, raw materials or finished product, marketable stocks or bonds, and such other sundry items as may be readily converted into money. Quick liabilities consist of current accounts payable, notes to the bank or to others for borrowed money, and such other sundry items as represent an obligation payable on demand or in the very near future. Slow-moving or dormant assets consist of real estate—whether occupied for business purposes or not, manufacturing plants, buildings, and such other sundries as cannot be readily converted into cash, or if converted must necessarily be heavily sacrificed to convert at all. Deferred liabilities against these items are usually mortgages on real estate or plant, bonded debt, or any other funded long-time obligation.

By making this segregation of quick assets and quick liabilities as against slow-moving assets and deferred liabilities it is easier to determine if the applicant will be able to meet obligations at maturity. Many a concern has become financially embarrassed because of too heavy an investment in real estate, which capital if not so invested would have enabled them to make a greater profit and pay their obligations more promptly had they rented the real estate; and if the real estate is encumbered with a mortgage, or the plant has a bonded debt, and the quick liabilities equal or exceed the quick assets the time will come when that institution must have an extension or seek new capital. In this connection it is advisable to ascertain if a large proportion of notes have been rediscounted at the bank, because the contingent liability of such rediscounts, especially if credits have been laxly granted, may seriously embarrass the applicant for credit in case the maker defaults on the notes so endorsed or discounted.

There is a wide difference of opinion among credit men as to what is the proper proportion of assets to liabilities, and no fixed rule has ever been established or recommended by any organization of credit men, though every well-seasoned credit man has fixed in his own mind some proportion beyond which it is dangerous to go. I have known credit men who would not as a rule extend credit if the total liabilities equalled 50% of the total assets; others will extend credit if the total liabilities equal 65% of the assets, and in some special lines of business credit men may be found who will even exceed that limit if the turnover is quick, the terms short and the concern has an established reputation for making prompt payments. Every credit man should, however, analyze the business he is engaged in and fix in his mind some proportion of liabilities to assets beyond which it is dangerous to extend credit.

It is well to remember too that every business requires a certain amount of capital, especially liquid capital, and if the owners of the business have not furnished enough capital they are going to try to use some of yours and the capital of their other creditors to finance the business until such time as the profits have accumulated and their capital thereby increased to such a point that the business can be properly conducted. Also, if the bank loans have been constant, or if they have been increasing, an analysis may show that the concern has always relied on renewals at the bank, and have done so for such a period of time that they regard the loan from the bank as a part of their fixed capital.

Distinction should be drawn between those concerns carrying a constant line of credit at the bank and those who carry even heavy loans at certain seasons to conduct their business but who liquidate those loans at certain seasons when the tide turns; for instance, a farmer will borrow heavily from the bank for various purposes to produce a crop, but when the crop has been produced and marketed the loan is paid off. On the other hand, if a mercantile institution borrows money from the bank and when the height of its season arrives and it should have made its collections and it has not paid off the loan, there is great danger that the loan may be considered or treated by the borrower as part of his fixed capital, and some day when the bank wants its money, which they surely will, and begin crowding the borrower unbeknown to the other creditors, that customer begins to take a little longer time on his current obligations in the hope that he can pay off his bank loan, and may even succeed in paying the loan off, thus leaving the creditors carrying the burden that the bank has been carrying.

Another important thing to watch is to see that loans have not been heavy from relatives, or that individuals of a corporation have not too heavily advanced personal funds payable on demand. They are in a position to secure themselves, seeing pending dangers first, and have every advantage over the ordinary creditor, and heavy loans made to a corporation by its stockholders, or by members of the family of an individual owning the business, should be regarded with suspicion.

Intangible assets of unknown quantity, such as patterns, good will, unsold treasury stock, and assets of like character should be practically disregarded as an asset in analzing financial statements.

Another thing to be considered carefully is whether your customer is conservative or speculative. A speculator may by a long chance accumulate wealth rapidly, but there is just as great danger that he will lose what he has accumulated by some plunge or an error in judgment. The conservative man who does not overextend, nor plunge long into undeveloped mining ventures, nor play the market—whether in securities or merchandise—is by far a better credit risk than an applicant with gambling instincts.

It is well to determine what the market for the product of your prospective customer is also. If the market is general and the competition is keen, credit must naturally be extended more cautiously than if the prospect has a monopoly or very little competition. This is especially so in the manufacturing business. A new concern with keen competition starting to manufacture an article, with unknown costs, and possibly working on misleading figures as to cost, unless there is ample capital behind the business, should be dealt with cautiously. On the other hand, a farmer may default in his obligation one year, and may even have a total crop failure, but if he owns his land his creditors can carry him over the next year, and even the next year, as he is sure to work out, assuming that he is honest and that his land is fertile and that he has not met with some catastrophe.

Furthermore, the general prosperity of the community is a factor in analyzing a financial statement. A concern doing business in a poorly populated territory, or in an agriculatural section where crop failures are frequent, is very likely to have difficulties; whereas a concern located in a community that has had a long period of prosperity and is not subject to droughts, transportation difficulties or labor troubles is, when other factors are good, a very satisfactory credit risk.

Lastly, the credit man should require information as to the insurance carried. If there is no fire insurance carried by the applicant for credit, a fire may wipe him off the map, and if the business depends upon the personal activity of individuals their lives should be insured in favor of the business for at least enough to enable that concern to pay its creditors should the mainstay of the business come to the end of life's journey. Also, workmen's compensation insurance should be carried in the proper amount, and contractors and others who are engaged in an extra hazardous business should carry public liability insurance. In the absence of these forms of insurance some disaster might occur which might seriously embarrass and might bankrupt many institutions that were fairly well established.

If possible, it is well to ascertain also how frequently the stock is turned over, which can quickly be measured by ascertaining the annual sales and the inventory. If stock is turned over slowly, obsolete stock accumulates and the inventory value depreciates correspondingly.

If the credit man will get information of the above character from reliable sources and weigh it carefully, he will not find much difficulty in reading the financial condition of his customer and determining whether credit can be safely extended or not.

CHAPTER IX

CONDITIONAL SALES CONTRACTS

The common expression "conditional sale" is now generally accepted as meaning a sale made on condition that title does not pass until the buyer has fully paid the purchase price. There may be other conditions in such a conditional sales contract, but the main condition is that the seller reserves title. If one parts with the ownership of anything, legally it is a sale, but if he parts with merely the possession and still retains the ownership, by agreement, it is a conditional sale. Legally the possession is transferred while the ownership is withheld until all deferred payments are completed, but of course, economically it is nevertheless a grant to the purchaser to utilize the commodity sold subject to the prior economic right of the seller to have returned to him a certain sum of money. By the condition of the contract, however, if that certain sum of money is not returned the seller has the right to retake the property, even though it be in the hands of another at the time of default.

A vast amount of sales are made in this country every day that could not otherwise be made if it were not for the protection afforded to the seller by the use of conditional sales. Many wage earners could not enjoy pianos, victrolas, sewing machines and other useful and necessary articles for home use were it not for this instrument, and even farmers and small industrials might not be able to expand as rapidly if they could not buy their implements or equipments on the installment plan, furnishing only as security a conditional sales contract, paying but a small proportion of the purchase price at the time of acquiring the property.

Conditional contracts of sale are valid as between the original parties thereto, if properly executed, without recording or filing, in every state, but to protect the seller's title as against third parties who otherwise might acquire some right or interest in the property without knowledge of the existing contract, it is necessary in some states to record or file such contract to give legal notice to all third parties of the real ownership of the property involved.

The requirements as to recording or filing vary in different states, but if properly executed and recorded or filed, as the law provides, they are an absolute protection to the seller as against nearly all third parties until the goods are paid for. The only exceptions are:

1. If the buyer is engaged in the business of reselling such articles, or using them in the course of manufacture, or in some other way by which they must necessarily be consumed or destroyed or lose their identity.

2. In some instances when the property becomes firmly attached or affixed to real estate and cannot be removed without serious damage to the real property.

3. In Illinois, where contracts of sale are not recognized even if recorded or filed, providing the rights of third parties are involved.

4. In Louisiana, where such contracts are not valid as against third parties and where a lease with an option to purchase, or a chattel mortgage, should be used.

5. In Pennsylvania, where a bailment contract or lease, with an option to purchase, is the proper form, unless the personal property becomes affixed to real estate.

6. In some few states, where the courts have held that the destruction of the property before it is fully paid for relieves the purchaser of further liability.

7. In a few others states, where the courts have held that the taking of independent security or the discounting of notes representing deferred payments operates to pass title.

8. Or in rare instances, where the seller was negligent in enforcing the payment or recovering the property and has become guilty of laches, resulting in the loss of his title rights.

The character of the article sold largely determines the advisability of using a conditional sales contract. For instance, furniture, sewing machines, pianos, musical instruments, automobiles, bicycles, machinery, and similar articles sold on the installment plan can be sold on a conditional sales contract. On the other hand, foodstuffs, articles for domestic consumption or articles consumed in manufacture cannot be satisfactorily sold on a title retaining contract.

There is a distinction between recording and filing these contracts. The object in each case is to give notice to third parties, but when a contract is recorded it must be copied in a book kept by the recording officer word for word and must be indexed properly, for which the recorder makes a service charge depending upon the amount of labor required. The filing of the same contract merely requires that a copy of the same be placed in the keeping of the officer designated by law and indexed for ready reference, in which case the fees are nominal.

In many states it is not necessary to either record or file the contract to make it valid as to all parties if it is in writing and properly signed. Other states have laws that require the recording or filing of the contract to make it valid, but it must also be in writing and properly signed, and in some states must be acknowledged by the purchaser or seller, and in some states must be witnessed. Other states require renewal or refiling after a certain period in order to preserve title.

There are very few states that impose a criminal liability upon the buyer for disposing of the property before it is paid for, but it may be noted that the status of property held under a conditional sales contract is rather peculiar. Under the terms of the contract the title remains in the seller until after all of the purchase price has been paid. However, from an equitable viewpoint the buyer acquires an interest in the property with his first payment and his interest increases with every installment that he has paid, and it is apparently for this reason that the legislatures of the various states and the courts take the view that there is no crime committed by the buyer in disposing of unpaid for property purchased on a conditional sales contract.

However, there are a few states prescribing a criminal penalty for disposing of property of this character before it is paid for. Many states, however, do provide a penalty if property held by the buyer is disposed of before a chattel mortgage given by him as part of the purchase price is fully satisfied.

Briefly stated, the requirements of the different states with respect to conditional sales contracts are outlined in the Appendix, though it is well to bear in mind that the requirements are often changed and a credit man should keep up to date, regardless of whether changes occur by legislative enactments or through court decisions.

In case of default in payment on the part of the buyer of any property purchased under a conditional sales contract the seller usually has two remedies, and in many states he must elect as to which of the two he will pursue. In many states if the seller elects to collect his claim by bringing action, the bringing of an action and the securing of a judgment automatically passes title. In most cases it is better for the seller to recover his property and resell, and in many states this can be done without legal process and with scant formality of any kind. The agent of the seller merely takes possession and that ends the transaction. But, of course, if the buyer opposes the taking of the property legal action is necessary, usually by way of replevin or foreclosure.

From a wide experience in dealing with conditional sales contracts, the writer has formed an impression that it is the tendency of the courts to protect the buyer as much as they can in case of default, and this is natural, as otherwise unscrupulous sellers would immediately upon default take possession of property that had been almost entirely paid for. On the other hand, there are unscrupulous buyers that would take advantage of sellers, and the form of a contract that does not clearly set forth all conditions and rights of the parties in case of default lessens the seller's security. Sellers of machinery probably meet with more technical difficulties than sellers of other classes of property. Several forms of conditional sales contracts are shown in the Appendix, covering machinery and other classes of personal property.

Credit men should train their salesmen to see that all conditional sales contracts are in proper form, that there is no ambiguity in the terms of payment and that the contract is properly executed by the buyer. Frequently the buyer is a corporation, and in case of controversy the seller might be called upon by the attorney for the buyer to prove that the individual executing on behalf of the buyer had authority to so execute. For this reason salesmen should be taught to insist that the individual signing for a corporate buyer show his authority for signing. This will indicate to the credit man whether that individual does have authority to make the purchase.

The sale of goods under conditional sales contracts covers such a broad field, and so many intimate questions arise, that no attempt has been made to give a complete analysis of the situation in all states; but credit men can always ascertain the laws of the states in which they are doing business covering the various phases of conditional sales, and if the credit man's field covers the entire United States there are several digests of the subject that will be of assistance in the solving of problems that arise daily.

CHAPTER X

TRADE ACCEPTANCES

There has been much interest displayed recently in the use of Trade Acceptances, and many educational campaigns have been started through the efforts of the Federal Reserve Banks, the American Trade Acceptance Council, and individual institutions who realize their value.

On the other hand, there are prejudices to overcome—prejudices existing not only in the mind of the dealer, but also in the minds of some bankers. This is natural, however, as every deviation from definite channels in the progress of the world has always met with opposition. For several years after automobiles came into use certain classes of people sneered at the owner of one, and a man who drove a car was regarded as a "snob" and not even entitled to the use of the highways. The automobile has, however, proven its worth, and so, regardless of prejudices and scepticism, the Trade Acceptance will prove its worth in American business.

The Federal Reserve Board in its circular of July, 1915, defines a Trade Acceptance as "A bill of exchange drawn to order having a definite maturity and payable in dollars in the United States, the obligation to pay which has been accepted by an acknowledgment, written or stamped, and signed, across the face of the instrument, by the company, firm, corporation or person upon whom it is drawn; such agreement to be to the effect that the acceptor will pay at maturity, according to its tenor, such a draft or bill without qualifying conditions."

The objections to the Trade Acceptance that it is not practical, that its use encourages inflation, or that it enables a certain class to obtain credit by juggling, or that it will drive out the practice of cash discounts, or that the details of making settlement through the use of Trade Acceptances are too burdensome, do not seem to stand the test of careful consideration.

Likewise the exponents of the use of Trade Acceptances may have hurt their cause by overstating the advantages. It is a mistake to say that the Trade Acceptance is the only proper instrument of credit, or that it will drive out the use of promissory notes and abolish the cash discount system, and that it is the only form of settlement which shows patriotism.

Why is not a promissory note a proper instrument of credit under some circumstances just as much as a Trade Acceptance is a proper instrument of credit? Why should Acceptances drive promissory notes out of existence? Single-name and two-name notes will always have a function in our credit relations. Why should a man who sells his goods for cash be expected to use Trade Acceptance involving long time credits, unless his cash discount is so heavy that he can better afford to do it? And why is a man who promptly pays an obligation less the cash discount not as patriotic as the man who passes up the cash discount and settles with Trade Acceptances?

Taking a broad view, therefore, it seems ridiculous to claim that the Trade Acceptance, as stated by many, is or will be the only satisfactory medium of settlement, and it is equally as ridiculous to deny that hundreds of millions of dollars' worth of goods sold on open accounts which if converted into Trade Acceptances would make for better business and benefit both buyer and seller.

Just at this time the American Trade Acceptance Council is authority for the statement that there are over four thousand firms in the United States who have adopted the use of Trade Acceptances, and these firms include almost every line of business. Of course, that there is a considerable advantage to the seller no one will deny. He can immediately convert into active capital funds that would otherwise be tied up in open book accounts. His banker should prefer to take his acceptance rather than his note, for it is not always easy to trace where the money went on a loan represented by a note, but a Trade Acceptance is positively known to represent a current transaction in the absence of fraud. Therefore, the seller has a liquid asset on which he can readily realize at the bank if he can convert his open book accounts into Trade Acceptances.

Some bankers have claimed that they prefer to buy promissory notes rather than Trade Acceptances because they then feel obliged to carefully analyze the statements of the maker of the note; that if the same firm issued a Trade Acceptance they would be more likely to rely on the double-named paper without as carefully analyzing the condition of the buyer as they would if they were advancing funds on his note. Some bankers also claim that unscrupulous borrowers might manufacture accommodation Acceptances. Other bankers have urged that they would not care to buy single-name paper of a borrower if he were in the habit of selling his Acceptances, because the holder of the Acceptances would have a lien upon the accounts receivable represented by such Acceptances. And it must be evident that both of these opposite views cannot be correct, one banker insisting that he will not buy Trade Acceptances because he does not think they are safe enough, and the other insisting that he will not buy single-name notes of a man who obtain and sells Trade Acceptances because such Trade Acceptances are so safe that they give the holder thereof a first lien on the borrower's book accounts.

Neither of these arguments seems to be complete. One buying Acceptances should familiarize himself as thoroughly with the financial condition of the endorser of these Acceptances as he would if he were buying a single-name note of the same party. If the discounter of these Acceptances was extending credit laxly to his own customers, the endorser of the Acceptances might not lend much strength to the paper, and the purchaser should rely more largely upon the financial standing of the endorser of the Acceptances by thoroughly analyzing his financial statement.

Likewise taking and giving Trade Acceptances assists the banker or credit man to analyze a financial statement obtained by him, as such statements are cleancut. On the asset side is shown the exact amount available in liquid items, against which are outstanding liabilities, and if some of the Trade Acceptances are sold (shown as a contingent liability) the banker would always ascertain what the funds sought to be borrowed on notes were required for and would find that such funds were for material to be used in the process of manufacture or some similar purpose, unless the borrower was giving his acceptance for the purchase of that material, etc., in which case the Trade Acceptance would show as a liability. Therefore, the borrower who gives Acceptance for such purchases cannot deceive his banker as to the real purpose for which new funds are sought by bank loans.

Some institutions are fighting the Trade Acceptance because they wish to maintain their business on a cash basis—that is, they are willing to pay a relatively high premium to avoid the cares and risks of sales on credit. Every institution must determine that point for itself, and, most certainly, it is not contemplated that the Trade Acceptance should be used in a business where cash payments can be obtained from customers of that institution.

The real function of the Trade Acceptance is to benefit the institution who must by custom grant credit terms through open book accounts. There are really only two classes of business institutions that can reasonably object to Trade Acceptances, the first class being unreliable purchasers who do not care to be bound on a definite obligation to pay on a certain definite date, and this is one of the reasons why the seller ought to urge the use of the Acceptance most strongly; the other class of objectors being large firms, of great financial strength, who desire to preserve their position of advantage against their competitors. The large borrower by using its own note can obtain funds on more favorable terms than its smaller competitors, which means that it can finance its purchases and its sales on a more favorable basis. It has the advantage of a larger scope of business and a lower rate of interest. It is true the large institution might still further increase its business by using Trade Acceptances, but the small firms are benefited more in proportion than the large ones, and this would shorten the handicap that the large firm now enjoys.

One of the advantages in the use of Acceptances that seems to have overlooked is that it quickens the "turnover." Every individual business transaction passes through many motions. In these times particularly it is to the general interest that money put out for labor and material return as fast as it can to the producer when his goods are sold. Until this money does return to the producer he must rely on bank credit, and frequently he must adjust the scope of his operations to the speed with which this "turnover" can be completed.

Here the Trade Acceptance plays an important part. The manufacturer can discount the Trade Acceptance and obtain the money much sooner than he could by carrying the obligation as an open book acount, but even though he does not discount these Acceptances and holds them until maturity he can figure in a very definite way and deal with concrete elements, rather than estimates of what proportion of his accounts will be paid on certain dates, for it is certain that a written obligation in definite concrete form, as the Trade Acceptance is, will certainly be paid at maturity more often than the open book account with only an implied understanding as to maturity.

Some of the advantages to the buyer are that it improves his standing, because it shows prompt paying methods. Giving Acceptances prevents the buyer from overexpanding and overbuying, because he will realize when he has a definite record of his obligations and as to when they mature that he cannot overstock or overbuy without knowing where the money is coming from to pay for the Acceptances he gives for such purchases; and training him to be a more careful and intelligent buyer is bound to be reflected in his profits at the end of the year. Furthermore, it will check any tendency to use commercial credit as fixed capital, and this may save serious embarrassment at some time when credit relations with his banker are strained or not available just at the time when his creditors are insisting upon payment of obligations owing them.

The buyer is also trained to be a better collector; because he must meet certain definite obligations on certain definite dates he will require his customers to pay him their accounts so that he may meet his own maturing obligations, thus reducing his losses, as the more prompt collections are the less the hazard and the less the ultimate loss in bad accounts.

Either the National Association of Credit Men or the American Trade Acceptance Council will furnish all those inquiring with approved and satisfactory forms of Trade Acceptance literature that is helpful in conducting an educational campaign, and booklets, or the names of banks issuing booklets, on the subject, that are very instructive and interesting.

CHAPTER XI

GENERAL KNOWLEDGE OF LAW AND INFORMATION ON CREDIT CONDITIONS

It is very helpful to a credit man to have a general knowledge of commercial law, particularly that respecting the collection of obligations and respecting contingent liabilities. This is especially so if the credit man is in charge of the collection department. The main items with which a credit man should acquaint himself are laws relating to:

        Exemptions,
        Mortgages, both real and chattel,
        Deeds,
        Taxes,
        Claims against estates,
        Conditional sales,
        Promissory notes,
        Collateral notes,
        Endorsements,
        Acknowledgments,
        Affidavits,
        Assignments,
        Attachments,
        Community interests,

Dower rights,
Limitations,
Mechanic's liens,
Interest,
Judgments,
Deeds of trust,
Redemption,
Replevin,
Bulk sales law,
Warehouse receipts,
Bills of lading,
Wills,
Supplementary proceedings,
Bankruptcy,

It is not very satisfactory to be compelled to consult a lawyer concerning the ordinary affairs of commercial life, and while it is not desirable or necessary for a credit man to act entirely as an attorney for his employer, it is desirable that he be sufficiently acquainted with these matters to enable him to pass judgment on the ordinary case.

As a rule an attorney is not a good business man, but if a credit man knows the practical operation of the laws of the states in his territory, a claim will be in proper shape when it goes to an attorney, if it ever reaches one. For instance, if the average attorney is consulted as to the liability of an endorser, he will tell you whether or not the note must be protested, but a shrewd credit man will not consult an attorney on that point, but will have notes prepared with a printed waiver on the back thereof. Occasionally banks will fail to protest a note, even if instructed to do so, but if your promissory note forms have printed across the back thereof a statement that presentment, protest, notice of protest and demand are waived, and that an extension may be granted without notice to the undersigned, it will not be necessary to instruct banks to protest, the endorser in that case being liable without protest.

Likewise, if a credit man is familiar with the laws relating to chattel mortgages, he will know when a chattel mortgage is received whether it is in proper form. He will know whether or not any rights are lost failing to foreclose or take possession of the property promptly at maturity date. He will protect himself by taking the form of collateral note that permits the holder thereof to sell the security without any advertisement, demand or notice, instead of the usual form without such a waiver, requiring the holder thereof to proceed to sell the property, as in the case of a pledge.

By familiarizing himself with these general subjects, he will know what assets to strike out of a statement that are exempt. In many statements rendered by applicants for credit there is included the value of their home, which in most states is absolutely exempt. It is usually not very difficult to obtain a copy of the statutes, or some simple form of publication covering all these points.

By having this information before you, you are prepared to act promptly. Should one of your debtors become deceased, you can readily ascertain what the requirements are with reference to filing claims against the estate, and, in fact, by obtaining the blank form of claims against estates, you can fill it out and file it with the administrator, or do whatever is necessary to put it in line for payment without the necessity of consulting an attorney or incurring the expense of attorneys' fees and maintain your own control over the obligation, as well.

A knowledge of the operation of the bankruptcy laws is also desirable, and this can be obtained from a number of books on bankruptcy published for just such purpose and thoroughly indexed, from which a credit man can get all the practical information necessary concerning bankrupt estates and bankruptcy claims. A separate chapter will be devoted to the subject of bankruptcy in Part II of this book.

A credit man should realize the extent to which the goods sold by the house are guaranteed or warranted. Even in the absence of any guarantee or warranty there is always an implied warranty that the goods sold are sound and merchantable and free from defects. It is very important in selling machinery to limit this guarantee or warranty to the replacement of defective parts of machinery, as otherwise the contingent damages might be very heavy, and if the credit man is also in charge of the collection department, he will get all of the grief adjusting accounts that are tied up on claims for defects, etc., but he can reduce the amount of these troubles by having a knowledge of the law relating to warranties and seeing that the goods are sold with the proper warranty and that the firm is protected against unjust claims.

In some states there is no redemption from a sale under a trust deed, and if a credit man knows these elementary legal facts, he will insist upon a trust deed instead of a mortgage if there is no redemption from the trust deed, and by acquainting himself with the laws relating to the subjects herein suggested, he can determine for himself what form of security is best for the house, what mode of procedure is best in case he gets in trouble, and what compromise settlement should be undertaken in case of serious difficulties.

A summary of some of these questions can be found in either Bradstreet's or Dun's rating books, but it is better to get some publication that covers the whole field in the territory where the credit man has jurisdiction.

It is advisable for a credit man to keep thoroughly informed on all conditions affecting credits in the territory in which the firm is doing business, and it is really desirable to study credit conditions of the country as a whole, as frequently certain conditions will spread from one section of the country to the other. Outside of calamities, the three things that affect credit the most are financial conditions, as reflected by the banks, crop conditions and trade or industrial conditions.

To keep informed on financial conditions it is desirable to obtain from some reliable source a consolidated statement of the condition of banks periodically, showing deposits, loans and clearings. If you do not get this all ready through some medium, your local bank can tell you how to get it in the district you are interested in. It is also well to keep in touch with your banker, as he is usually well informed on all conditions affecting credit. Bank clearings, bank deposits and bank loans somewhat measure the activity of business, and a comparative statement will show whether the tendency is up or down.

In order to be informed on crop conditions there is nothing more dependable than the government crop report, and this is furnished free to those desiring it by the Department of Agriculture at Washington upon request, and if you do not receive the government crop reports now it is recommended that you write to the Department of Agriculture and get on the mailing list.

This is a complete crop report covering the United States, but the condition of crops by states or districts is also shown, as well as comparative data that is quite valuable. Other information concerning agricultural conditions in your immediate district should also be obtained, and this is comparatively easy to get, but full consideration should be given to it. For instance, if the season has been exceedingly dry and a short crop is expected, money will not be as easy as if a good crop was produced, market conditions being equal.

Trade and industrial conditions should be watched to the same extent. Dun's Weekly Review gives some very valuable information along these lines, and a credit man connected with a firm dealing largely with manufacturers must necessarily keep well informed on conditions of this sort.

In a mining district it is usually possible to get reliable data concerning the prosperity of the mining community in which you are interested, and where oil is produced it is desirable to follow closely the production and consumption figures. General local conditions should be watched carefully.

PART II

MERCANTILE COLLECTIONS

CHAPTER I

FUNCTIONS OF A GOOD COLLECTOR

The prime requisite of the manager of a collection department is to so conduct the department that obligations are collected at maturity. This sounds very simple, but in actual practice much difficulty is found in carrying out this duty properly. Of course, whether or not collections can be made promptly at maturity depends largely upon the policy followed by the credit manager. If the credit department is run separately, or if run by the same party in charge of collections, then the success in collecting promptly depends upon the policy pursued by this same party in the original extension of his credits. If it is the policy to be liberal in granting credits in order to get a large volume of business, and take some chances, collections will naturally be more difficult than if conservative judgment is exercised and credit extended only to those whose financial condition is such as will enable them to pay promptly.

A good collector should make as few enemies as possible, and drastic or rough-shod methods are only to be resorted to in extreme or emergency cases, after having ascertained that the ordinary, usual, courteous business methods are not sufficient—in fact, a collector has not really done good work if he has collected a slow account and left some substantial customer in such a frame of mind that he will never again do business with the firm. There are many concerns throughout the country who are amply solvent, but merely slow pay. Many of them lack business courtesy, and pay very little, if any, attention to requests for payment. After writing two or three times a collector gets exasperated and proceeds to press the account vigorously. However, care and thought should be used in determining on a course to be followed, as frequently diplomatic methods will bring about collection faster than harsh methods would, and enable a collector to still retain for the benefit of his firm the good will of the delinquent.

A good collector should use constructive methods, and if a debtor is involved make suggestions that will enable him to get on his feet so that he can pay you. It is far better to give him the benefit of your business judgment so that he can pay you, rather than be compelled to liquidate, which not only puts him out of business, but which probably will cause your firm a loss, as very few concerns liquidate and pay one hundred cents on the dollar.

The application of constructive methods involves a careful analysis of the reasons why your customer is not paying at maturity. The first requisite is to get his confidence. After you have a debtor's confidence and can get a complete statement of his business, you can determine where the trouble is, and unless the case is a hopeless one suggest methods for overcoming that trouble. In getting this statement you can also determine whether it is advisable to insist on security.

Extensions should be granted only for an adequate consideration. It is usually not the best practice to grant an extension when a debtor merely asks for it, without showing any specific reason as to why it is necessary, and in most cases it is better to obtain security; or if an open account is to be extended, it is recommended that a promissory note be taken, payable at the time the extension would mature, and, if necessary, the note should be endorsed. In some cases it is desirable to take a collateral note, with an assignment of certain accounts owing the debtor as collateral security. But whatever form the extension takes it should be only for a sufficient consideration. Following that rule is one of the best plans in existence to cure debtors from continually asking extensions just because they think it may not be entirely convenient to pay the account at maturity. The collector should endeavor to teach all the debtors of his institution that an obligation is definite and concrete and that payment is always expected at maturity.

Another function of the collector is to assist in promptly adjusting complaints. Many of the complaints come to the collection department for adjustment, unless there is a regularly ordained complaint department to dispose of such matters. However, it is the tendency of debtors to hold up the entire obligation if they have even a minor complaint. Not only should you assist in undertaking to satisfactorily adjust the complaint, but pending adjustment a letter should be sent to the debtor stating that his claim is receiving attention and that in the meantime it is requested that he send in a remittance for a portion of the account. That is to say, if a man owes a thousand dollars past due and holds up the entire balance because of some complaint that does not aggregate more than fifty or sixty dollars, it is desirable to write to him suggesting that he send in nine hundred dollars on account and allow the other one hundred dollars to stand until his complaint is adjusted. This very materially assists in making most adjustments, as many of them are largely imaginary, and the more money a customer owes, the more complaint he thinks he has; and, conversely, the less he owes, the less he thinks his complaint is.

Regardless of the business transacted, and regardless of the form of the obligation, some notification should be given the debtor on the day of maturity or shortly before the obligation matures. In the case of open accounts the usual custom is to send a statement of the open account as it appears on the ledger. Some concerns render a statement showing the balance due on

FUNCTIONS OF A GOOD COLLECTOR

the 1st of the preceding month, to which is added the date and the amount of each purchase during the current month, and from the total is subtracted credits for goods returned, allowances made and cash paid. Other concerns prefer to list every unpaid item on the statement instead of showing the balance due on the 1st of the month, so that the collection department will have their attention drawn to old items, which may be overdue and which might not be so noticeable if the statement were rendered by merely showing the balance due on the 1st of the month. Unless the purchases and credits are too voluminous on each account it is recommended that statements be rendered showing all unpaid items, not only to call the attention of the collection department to such unpaid items past due, but so that the attention of the debtor himself may be forcibly drawn to the fact that many of his purchases are long past due.

Where the obligation is in the shape of a note a notice should be sent to the debtor before maturity so that he will have an opportunity to pay it at maturity. Of course, if a promissory note is delivered to some bank for collection, the bank will send a printed notice of maturity to the debtor, filling in the amount of the note and the day it falls due. If the note is not discounted or sent through a bank for collection, and the notice of maturity is given to the debtor by the creditor direct, a printed form should be used and mailed to the debtor so that it will reach him about ten days before maturity, or long enough before maturity to give him an opportunity to have a remittance in the hands of the creditor, or his agent, at maturity, being either more or less than ten days before maturity. This printed notice should provide a space to show the date the note was given, the amount of the principal, the accrued interest to date of maturity, and directions as to where funds should be sent to liquidate the obligation and where the promissory note is held for collection.

If business done is by contract and under the terms of the contract certain payments fall due at certain specified times, or when certain work has been completed to a certain stage, as in the case of buildings, machinery being built to order, etc., a special letter is, of course, necessary to notify the debtor the amounts due on certain dates in accordance with the contract.

If according to the terms of sale payment is due on delivery or upon presentation of shipping documents, for which a draft is drawn with the bill of lading attached, the holder of the draft for collection will send a proper notice, but many firms follow the practice of sending a notice direct to the buyer that a draft is forwarded with shipping documents attached. There is some advantage in this practice, in that it shows your customer that you are giving him good service, and, also, so that in case the holder of the draft neglects to send the notice, or in case the notice is misdirected or lost, the buyer will nevertheless have advice from the seller that the obligation is due and he will then know when to expect the arrival of the material.

Trade acceptances are usually discounted or turned over to a bank for collection, and in that case the bank can be depended upon to send notice of maturity, as such paper is always payable at some specified bank.

CHAPTER II

FOLLOW-UP SYSTEM AND COLLECTION LETTERS

The best collectors are the most persistent; the most persistent collectors are the most systematic.

An easygoing collector soon loses all hold and control of his debtors; but one who has a reputation of being strict, yet fair and considerate, gets results with the least effort and makes the least losses; in fact, if credit is extended with a reasonable amount of judgment, barring calamities, most accounts are collectible at or about maturity. The losses usually creep in through laxness and by not persistently pressing debtors for payment at maturity, and with much vigor thereafter.

To follow collections closely it is necessary to have a follow-up system, and this system should be as nearly automatic as possible. One effective method is to have an extra copy of the customers' monthly statements furnished to the collection department, and these can be gone over by stenographers or clerks in the office, and those which have not matured eliminated. Those which have matured can be classified and certain form letters written those in a certain class. The copy of the statement should be kept, and on it should be noted what form was sent; or if a special letter is sent, a carbon copy of the letter should be attached to the statement. This starts the file as soon as the account is due. On the carbon copy of the letter should be marked the date that the collector desires this particular matter to come up for attention again. That carbon should then be filed ahead in the date marked thereon. In this way each day there is placed on the collector's desk from the filing department all matters coming up for attention that day. Clerks may run through these files and eliminate items that have been paid. If the number of accounts being followed is voluminous, and it is desired to keep correspondence in alphabetical order, or if a number system of filing is used and it is desired to keep that follow-up letter in its proper place in the file, then a card should be made out with the name of the debtor and the date upon which the matter is to be brought up written thereon by the stenographer or filing clerks, and such cards should be put ahead in the file on the date noted, so that a stenographer or file clerk may get out all these files on each day as they come up. These follow-up matters should be carefully checked over before a follow-up letter is sent out to be sure that no debtor is being pursued for payment after he has already paid.

If the names of debtors are taken off on a list when the trial balance is taken, an extra copy of such list should be made, to be used as a collection list on which can be noted the payments made each day opposite the customer's name. If this is done systematically every night, the collection department will have before them each morning a complete list of the customers, with their accounts as of the 1st of the month brought up to date in so far as payments are concerned.

If the organization of the cashier's department is such that this collection list can be gotten out and the payments noted thereon they are very helpful and well worth the effort required to keep them written up daily.

Special lists of accounts 60 or 90 days or more past due should always be on the collector's desk, and if the work is segregated among several collectors, alphabetically or otherwise, this should be divided so that accounts 60 or 90 days or more overdue are always before the collector in charge of the collection thereof, and as payments come in on these accounts they should be stricken off, and this special list should be analyzed every day as well as the analysis they get through the follow-up system. Vigorous campaigns should be directed toward the collection of such older accounts.

Following the maturities of notes is substantially the same as following open accounts, except that no statement is prepared, but a memorandum should be given the collector by the bookkeeping department or cashier, showing the maturity of notes about ten or fifteen days before they mature, and if they are not paid promptly at maturity the collector should immediately take such items up for collection, and as with accounts, notes that are 90 days or more overdue should be carefully listed and given very special attention.

No special collection letter forms are outlined herein, for it is better if a collector can devise his own form of letter to meet the circumstances of the case, using his own individual style of diction, the individuality of which will probably get better results than some stereotyped form of letter that may be generally used by several collectors and the general tone of which will appeal to the debtor as being a stock form.

The writing of effective collection letters is an art, and the thought should always be borne in mind that you wish to attract the debtor's attention to the letter in the opening sentence, so that it will not be thrown aside without receiving due and proper attention; in other words, you have a message to deliver and it is important to get the immediate attention of the debtor in order to deliver that message. The "ding dong" type of letter is practically worthless. Many collectors make the mistake of writing the same old stuff month in and month out to delinquent debtors and then wonder why they cannot succeed in collecting certain old accounts; for instance, at times on an old delinquent account you can catch the debtor's attention by using as an openingسentence, "Have you an order for us?" Frequently this surprises the delinquent and the thought occurs to him that the firm must appreciate his business after having carried him so long to solicit him for an order, and in many cases he will actually remit the old account whether he places an order or not. If he does remit and sends an order also, the order can be dealt with according to existing circumstances and the condition of his finances; if he sends an order and does not remit, it gives the collector an opportunity of writing him, if the occasion requires it, that the order is received and is having attention, but cannot be filled until the past due account is paid.

Short letters are the most effective. A man can grasp the contents of a short letter in a hurry, but if an effort is required to read a long one, it is cast aside until more leisure time is had for reading it. Catchy expressions are also of an advantage at times; also, pretexts are frequently helpful; for instance, in the summer season at vacation time frequently a debtor is amused and his attention is attracted by an opening sentence, as follows: "Will you help me get my vacation?" This sentence can be followed by stating that, if so, a customer can remit by a certain time, when the collector expects to go on his vacation. It is rarely ever a good practice so far as effectiveness is concerned to beseech a customer to pay—positive statements are always more fruitful of results. A dictator should adopt a mental attitude in writing collection letters that prompt attention is expected, and that thought should permeate the whole letter; in fact, the closing portion of it should state that prompt attention is expected.

As a general rule, also, it is not an effective method to speak too much of a favor on the part of the debtor in case he remits. He should instead be impressed with the fact that he is in arrears on obligations, and in many instances good results can be obtained by calling attention to the fact that if his orders were neglected by the firm as his accounts are being neglected, he would not have a very good opinion of the house. Some collection campaigns should have for their theme with certain classes of delinquents that failure to pay the obligation has been due to carelessness or oversight. In that case, sending a duplicate statement with a self-addressed envelope enclosed is frequently effective. There is a great deal of suggestion conveyed in the sending of a self-addressed envelope. This suggestion may be further impressed upon the debtor's mind by the use of a blank check, which will be referred to in a later chapter.

Terse, snappy, forceful letters should be used, rather than long, verbose, repetitive, unimpressive, formlike letters. The debtor should be impressed more with his sense of individual responsibility, his sense of obligation, his sense of duty or neglect of duty and the mutuality involved, rather than imbued with the thought that when he does pay his account he is extending some favor, and the strain of letters should be such as to endeavor in every way possible to cure the customer of the thought that every time he is pressed for money on an obligation that he ought to pay without pressure, all that it is necessary for him to do is to indicate that he will transfer his business elsewhere. The collector should give his letters a distinctive, individual appearance, and they should be full of ginger.

CHAPTER III

UNUSUAL, UNIQUE AND RESOURCEFUL METHODS

It is necessary that a successful credit man or collector should be resourceful. Frequently an unexpected condition has arisen suddenly in the debtor's affairs that strikes consternation in the heart of his creditors and cause no end of concern to the credit man or collector representing an institution holding a claim against such debtor. Even though a man may be well poised he is apt to get panicky, and the fear of loss may jeopardize his ability to use calm and deliberate judgment, or interfere with his ability to determine just what is the best course to pursue.

One of the greatest attributes one exercising the function of a collector can have is foresight—not in the sense of having the foresight of a prophet, nor in the sense that future contingencies must be forecasted, but in the sense that if given all the present facts concerning the finances, obligations and operations of a business, what the probable condition of that business will be at a certain time in the future. The time to weigh this condition thoroughly is at the time of default in payment. If full information shows there is some justifiable explanation or reason for default which is of a temporary character and which in the usual course of events will be almost certain to be overcome, there is no great cause for alarm; but if knowledge of all existing facts shows a danger signal ahead, the credit man or collector is then obliged to promptly use his forethought and judgment.

Some suggestions are offered in this chapter as to ensuring the ultimate payment of an obligation from an involved debtor by obtaining security. The line of approach must naturally and necessarily be largely determined by the existing circumstances, the character of the business and other varying factors. For this reason the suggestions here offered are not offered in the order that should be followed in an attempt to obtain the necessary security, but are offered in addition to some of those usually followed, existing circumstances to determine which of the suggestions, if any, should be tried out on the defaulting debtor.

The usual defaulting debtor owes an open account. If the credit man or collector feels that an extension can be safely granted on such an account for a definite time, with reasonable assurance that at the end of the extension the debtor will be able to meet his engagement, either an unsecured or an endorsed promissory note may be accepted, bearing interest. Experience has shown this is a good general rule to follow. The execution of a note impresses the debtor with the fact that the obligation must be met at the time he has agreed to pay it, if extended, and if there is any misgiving on his part as to his ability to pay the obligation when the extension has expired it will usually be voiced at the time the note is executed, for then the debtor is face to face with a very definite and concrete obligation. Furthermore, he realizes the fact that he is being accommodated, and very few debtors will object to paying the current rate of interest for accommodation. Many credit men provide in the form of note used that the rate of interest shall be the prevailing current rate, but that after maturity the obligation shall draw interest at 12%, or even higher, so that in case the note must be carried after maturity the debtor must pay something more than a mere prevailing market rate to money borrowers. This is natural, as merchants are not in the banking business.

A promissory note should also be taken from the contentious type of debtor if he seeks an extension. Many complaints are made on a pretext to gain time, and if it is thought the part of wisdom to grant the extension sought, a note should be taken to forever cut off any further claim from that debtor. Furthermore, if legal action should be required later, it is a simple matter to prove up the obligation in court if it is in the form of a promissory note, the only real defense to a promissory note being lack of consideration or fraud, whereas proving the order, shipment or receipt of the goods on a long open book account is in case of a contest, often difficult.

The note should in all cases provide that the debtor should pay attorney's fees,—either 10% of the principal or a statement that he is obligated to pay all attorney's fees accrued in the collection thereof. Such an obligation on the part of the debtor may not be legally enforced in all jurisdictions, but in most states such a condition in a note has been held to be good; even, however, where there may be some question about such a provision it is desirable to have it in the note, as many debtors are not aware of the legality of such a clause, and it furnishes a credit man with a wonderful argument to be able to say that he hopes the debtor will not compel him to place the matter in the hands of an attorney to enforce payment, which not only will add the burden of court costs to the debtor but compel him to pay for services of his attorney and also compel him to pay your attorney as well. Very few men are so obstinate, regardless of temperament, that they will deliberately permit a creditor to take legal action to enforce payment of a note when they know they are obliged to pay both the lawyer prosecuting the claim and the lawyer defending the claim and court costs as well. The following form of promissory note has been used and found satisfactory. Attention is called to the printed waiver on the back thereof, as this is a decided advantage to the creditor if the note is endorsed.

(NOTE FORM)

$............ .... 19... No.................
............after date for value received............promise to
pay to JOHN DOE & Co., Inc., or order at.......................
....
............................Dollars with interest from date
until paid, at the rate of...........................per cent
per annum, payable quarterly; and in case of default in payment
of interest when due, both principal and interest shall immediately
become due and payable at the option of the holder of this note.
Should this note be placed in the hands of an attorney for collection............agree to pay an additional sum of ten per cent on
principal as attorney's fees. Principal and interest payable in
gold coin of the United States.
Address ....
   "   ....
   "   ....

(WAIVER.) (On Back of Note)

I, (or we) hereby guarantee payment, jointly and severally, of the within note or any renewal or extension thereof and all expense of collection thereof and all expense incurred in enforcing this guaranty and waive demand, presentment for payment, protest, and notice of protest, and consent that the time for payment may be extended without notice to me (or us).

If it is determined that some security must be taken, a collateral note should be used. The character of security demanded may be stocks or bonds, or sometimes a bill of sale to personal property may be demanded as collateral, or a deed to real property. The average merchant does not usually have either stocks or bonds that he can furnish as collateral, and a bill of sale to personal property attached to a collateral note may not be enforcible. Nevertheless, if the bill of sale is recorded, collection may be enforced by selling the personal property as property under a chattel mortgage is sold but without as much legal procedure, and if the form of collateral note hereafter outlined is used, even a suit to foreclose may often be avoided.

Likewise a deed to real property attached to a collateral note may not be always legally enforcible without going through a foreclosure, but if the deed is recorded the property may always be foreclosed upon as though the instrument had been a mortgage, and if there is no definite agreement recited in the note in the form of a defeasance to the effect that the holder will return the deed when the obligation is paid, it is often possible to merely record the deed upon default in payment of the collateral note and acquire title to the property, by holding a sale, either public or private, in accordance with the terms of such note. Even, however, though it would not be legally possible to do this, the advantage obtained by taking this form of security instead of a chattel or real estate mortgage is that the debtor is likely unaware of his rights, and in the belief that unless he pays the obligation he will lose title to the personal property represented by the bill of sale, or lose title to the real property represented by the deed, with all his equity of redemption cut off, he will promptly discharge the obligation.

The form of collateral note to be used should be the broad form used by the larger banks, most of which are the same in tenor. Such forms provide that in the event of default the holder of the collateral may sell the security without any advertisement, demand or notice. Of course, it is not necessary for the credit man to follow any cut-throat practice and sell some debtor out in a harsh manner, but the holding of security in that form will enable you to make collection much quicker than if you were obliged to go through the formality of selling the security by demand, advertisement and notice as a pledge. Furthermore, the very publicity of the sale might be disastrous to all concerned; other creditors might be perfectly willing to extend time to this debtor, but thinking that some other creditors were taking advantage, or that they were selling out securities, they would take steps to have the debtor thrown into bankruptcy.

Such collateral note forms also provide that the holder may demand additional security if the value of the security, in the judgment of the holder thereof, falls below the amount of the obligation, or deems it to his interest to call for additional security, and the note form provides that in the event of a sale, any surplus, after deducting the cost of sale will be returned to the maker of the note; and the maker also is of course liable for any deficiency in the event that the security sold does not satisfy the obligation. The holder of the note credits on the note the amount realized from the sale of the securities and a judgment may be obtained for the deficiency.

A form of collateral note which has been found to meet all conditions, and which is good for all purposes, follows:

(NOTE)

No. ....
$............   Chicago, Ill., ... 19...
.....................................after date, for value received, I promise to pay to the order of JOHN DOE & Co., at....
....
....Dollars,
with interest at the rate of........................per cent, per annum from date until paid.

Sign
....
Here

The undersigned has deposited with said John Doe & Co., as collateral security for the payment of the above note, and of every other liability or liabilities, either direct or contigent, now owing or which may hereafter be owing, whether now or hereafter contracted, of the undersigned to said payee, or to the legal holder thereof, the following property, viz.:

....
....
....
....

With the right on the part of the said John Doe & Co., or the legal holder hereof from time to time to call for additional security of such kind and value as will be satisfactory to said John Doe & Co., or the legal holder hereof, and on failure to respond, or if in the judgment of said John Doe & Co., or the legal holder hereof, said security, or any additions thereto or substitutes therefor or any part thereof, shall have depreciated in value, then the whole of the above note shall be deemed immediately payable at the election of the said John Doe & Co. or the legal holder hereof, with full power in said John Doe & Co., or the legal holder hereof on maturity thereof, either by its terms or by election as aforesaid, or on the non-payment of any of the other liabilities above mentioned, to at any time, and from time to time, sell, assign and deliver the whole of said property and all additions thereto and substitutes therefor, or any part of said property, additions and substitutes, at any public or private sale, at the option of said John Doe & Co., or the legal holder hereof, and without advertising the same and without notice to the undersigned, and with the right of said John Doe & Co., or the legal holder hereof, to be a purchaser at any public sale or sales; and in the event of any sale or purchase hereunder no matter by or to whom made, all notice thereof, and any and all equity or right of redemption, whether before or after sale hereunder is hereby expressly waived; and, after deducting all legal and other costs and expenses, including reasonable attorneys fees, from the proceeds of such sale or sales, to apply the remainder on any one or more of said liabilities, whether due or not, as said John Doe & Co., or the legal holder hereof shall deem proper (making rebate of interest on any demands not matured), and return the surplus, if any, to the undersigned. Said John Doe & Co., or the legal holder hereof, may at its, his or their discretion enforce the collection of said security, additions thereto and substitutes therefor by suit or otherwise, and may surrender, compromise, release, renew, extend or exchange all or any of the same. Said John Doe & Co., or the legal holder hereof is hereby authorized and empowered at any time to apply to the payment of any liability or liabilities, whether the same be due or not, of the undersigned, to said John Doe & Co., or to the legal holder hereof, whether the same be due or not, all property real and personal, of every kind and description, including balances, credits, collections, moneys, drafts, checks, notes, bills, or accounts of the undersigned.

.... Sign Here

Address........................

The printed waiver on the back, eliminating protest, etc., may be the same as in the case of unsecured notes, outlined previously in this chapter, or may simply state:

"The undersigned endorsers hereby waive all presentation, demand, notice of non-payment, protest and notice of protest.

"........................
........................"

The average merchant, however, has his liquid assets most largely in the form of open book accounts, and it is to this form of security that the credit man or collector must generally look for protection. A practice which seems to be very rarely followed is that of demanding a collateral note with an assignment of certain of the debtor's accounts against his customers as collateral. Assignments of accounts in that form are valid in practically every jurisdiction. The debtor need not be embarrassed with his customers, because it is not usually necessary to notify the customer of the debtor that you hold an assignment of the account and that remittance must be made to you. The debtor's customers can make remittance direct to the debtor, but, of course, he (the debtor) is obliged to remit you, and in that sense he is virtually acting as your agent. He might be criminally liable if he failed to properly account for such collections. The usual assignment is as follows:

"FOR VALUE RECEIVED, I (or we) hereby sell, assign, transfer, and set over unto.. all my (our) right, title and interest in and to the within (or annexed, or foregoing) account."

........................,"
(Signature.)

If there is any question about the debtor's honesty or integrity, the collateral note can be deposited in some bank, together with the assigned accounts, and the customers of the debtor can be notified by the bank to remit to them. The margin of security on assigned accounts over the amount of the obligation owing by the debtor must be determined by the character of the business of the debtor. If he is known to be lax in extending credits, the margin should be larger than if he is conservative. If some of the obligations owing your debtor are in the shape of notes, he should endorse the notes over, and such notes should be attached to the collateral note as security, and their collection can be handled in the same way as the collection of assigned accounts is handled.

If the extension sought is short, and the debtor is known to be a good promiser but a poor executor of promises, it is desirable to suggest the giving of a postdated check. This might be resented by many debtors, but if diplomatically handled it should not be. The credit man or collector can say he is about to make up a report of past due accounts to the President or some other executive officer of the company and does not wish to show that particular account overdue, and that if a check is given dated a little ahead his name can be left off the list.

It is not very often that your customer will permit his check to be dishonored. If he does, your claim is a very much better one than when it was an open account, and while it is very rarely a criminal offense to default in payment on a post-dated check some debtors are not aware of this fact and will hasten to make good a check outstanding against them whether or not they are criminally liable, because they realize that there can be no greater reflection on their general credit than to have it reported that they failed to make good outstanding checks.

Occasionally a credit man or collector is found with a check on his hands that is returned unpaid—sometimes post-dated and sometimes bearing the current date, given in the ordinary course of business—with the reason for nonpayment endorsed by the bank "insufficient funds," and in many bankruptcy proceedings creditors are found holding checks dishonored for that very reason. A practice that seems to be little followed is that of determining how much short the check is, and then depositing to the credit of the debtor enough money to make the check good.

For instance, if you are given a check for $100.00, by diplomatically handling the matter with the bank you can find out how much the debtor's account is short. If you cannot discuss the matter with an out of town bank, possibly you can send the check to a traveling salesman and have him call at the bank and get him to ascertain how much the account is short. In the case recited, if you learn, for instance, that there is but $90.00 on deposit, while you have a $100.00 check, you can deposit $10.00 to the customer's credit, or have the traveling man do it, and the check will be cleared. Banks will not ordinarily state just how much money a customer of theirs has on deposit, but if it is stated to them that you hold a check drawn on them which has been returned unpaid by them and which you believe was issued by the maker of the check without having kept an accurate account of his balance at the bank, or due to an error in calculation on his part, and that you would like to protect him against a dishonored check, the bank will ordinarily tell you approximately how much money must be deposited to make the check good, or give you some idea of what the bank balance is.

The matter can be explained to your customer by assuring him that it was not your desire to have his credit hurt by having a dishonored check, so that you took the liberty of depositing enough money to his credit in the bank to make the check good. You can tell him that you have charged the cash advanced to his account and state that you realize he appreciates your thoughtfulness and ask that as soon as convenient he send you a remittance for the amount of cash you have laid out to protect his credit. In the case above recited, if he goes through bankruptcy before you collect the ten dollars cash advanced, you have a $10.00 claim against him instead of a $100.00 claim.

Even though, however, you may find the balance to be deposited is too great to make the check good, or even though you may be unable to find out from the bank how much must be deposited to make up the deficiency, you are in a very much better position in having a dishonored check as compared to having a past due open account, and the percentage of unpaid post-dated checks is small compared to those that are paid or those that can be made good by depositing a reasonable sum to cover the deficiency, and it is safe to say that most of the deposits made to cover those deficiencies are later taken care of. Furthermore, experience has shown that this procedure will demand the respect of your customers more than if you allowed them to become lax in the handling of their overdue account.

A great deal of difficulty is experienced in collecting small past due accounts, and the use of blank checks is often very helpful in making collection of such accounts. The practice followed is to have some blank checks printed with the name of the bank left blank, and with a stub attached, and the stenographer can fill out the check for the amount of the small account and date it, and fill out the stub, and enclose a self-addressed envelope, with a general form letter calling your customer's attention to the fact that all he need do is write in the name of his bank, sign check, enclose it in the self-addressed envelope and send it back. A letter transmitting this should be captioned, "A new service for our customers," or something similar, so that the debtor is impressed with the fact that this procedure is intended to better serve him and make it more convenient for him to pay. Those who do not sign the check and send it back, will usually send one of their own, and the work involved in filling out checks of this character by the stenographer is much less than trying to collect small past due accounts by the usual collection methods. A satisfactory form of blank check and stub is here shown:

CHECK STUB	........................19..
............19..	......................Bank,
To JOHN DOE & Co.	of.......................
For	Pay to JOHN DOE & Co., or Order, $......
....	............................Dollars.
....	....

Another procedure that is helpful in collecting past due accounts is to charge interest, and charge it monthly, and send the bill for the interest every month, and have it show on the statement every month. At times this procedure may irritate a debtor, and there may be cases where it is undesirable to follow the rule, but those customers who are exceedingly touchy, or who might withdraw their business if annoyed with monthly bills for interest, can be excepted. If some good customer is charged interest or sent interest bills and highly resents it, the matter can be explained as an oversight on the part of the bookkeeping department in going through the ledgers making up the monthly interest bills, by stating that it was an oversight to have included that particular account.

Obtaining an individual guarantee on an obligation already owing is substantially the same proposition as obtaining a guarantee on an account before time of shipment, excepting that there must be adequate consideration provable for the giving of a guarantee on an obligation that has already been incurred, as has been fully outlined in the chapter on the subject of guarantees. However, this is a form of security that a credit man or collector should not over-look in attempting to get an obligation in such shape as to insure ultimate recovery. If is not only desirable to see that the consideration for the giving of such a guarantee is sufficient, but it is a good rule to be sure that extensions of any character are given only for an adequate consideration—the consideration usually being some form of security.

If a debtor does not promptly respond to letters asking for security, the follow-up should be sent by registered mail. The fact that a letter is registered usually impresses the receiver thereof with the thought that it is valuable or requires special attention. Furthermore, he knows the sender is going to get a receipt showing that he received the letter. This cuts off any excuse for failure to respond. In some instances letters should be sent by special delivery, or they may be registered and a special delivery stamp attached also, which gives the receiver the idea that the matter is of extreme importance and must have prompt attention. If the delay might be too great in getting your follow-up message to the customer by registered letter, or special delivery letter, it is desirable to use the telegraph; or, if you have sent a registered letter or special delivery letter and have received no reply to that form of appeal, then a telegram should be sent demanding immediate attention. Not only is the debtor then brought face to face with a realization that you are insistent and positively demand that he give the matter attention, but he does not know but that the contents of the message may reach the eyes of others in a way that might still further embarrass him.

If all efforts to obtain security have failed, and the account is in a precarious condition, efforts should be made to offset the obligation by purchasing from the debtor something that can be resold. Such an offset, in the absence of fraud, is good, even if a bankruptcy petition should be filed shortly afterwards. For instance, if your customer runs a lumber mill, purchase the lumber even if you know you have no use for it and sell it at a slight discount if you anticipate a loss on his account; in fact, no matter what the debtor produces, or resells, if there is any reasonable market for it you can usually find that market and make a ready sale of the product by allowing some slight discount under the market. This is much better than to find your debtor is so involved that the account will drift along, with the prospect that you will ultimately face a much larger loss than the slight discount you know you will lose if you accept the wares of your customer to apply as a credit on your claim against him. This procedure will often enable you to realize even after some other creditor has obtained security.

If a debtor is contrary, some dummy may be induced to purchase some goods along these lines, and your claim can be assigned to the dummy. The dummy cannot be required by your customer to pay the same because he will have an offset against your customer in the shape of the account you assigned to him. This is a good suggestion to give to attorneys when they have claims against involved debtors in all cases where it would seem unwise to precipitate matters by commencing legal proceedings.

Should your customer later get on his feet he will likely appreciate the fact that you tried to help him out when he was involved, by trading out the account, and he should be glad to know when he was in trouble you helped him out by accepting his goods, on which he made a profit, towards the liquidation of his account, at a time when it would have seriously embarrassed him to have demanded payment in money.

Lost debtors may be traced in various ways. Some of the methods followed are to send a registered letter to the last known address, with a demand for a return card, and the return card will show when it gets back, the postmark of the city at which the letter was delivered, even though the debtor may have moved away. This is especially so if the registered letter is marked "deliver to addressee only," for then the postoffice will not deliver the registered letter to any other members of the debtor's family or to any of his agents. Lost debtors may sometimes be traced through business associates, through relatives, or through a personal advertisement in the newspapers.

The foregoing suggestions will probably call to the mind of the credit man or collector other resourceful methods that the circumstances of the case will indicate as being the proper ones to pursue, but the most satisfactory rule is to require some form of security on the account as soon as there is a default in payment. On the obtaining of security an extension should be granted in a definite way and not permit the delinquent to get the impression that the account can run along, even though secured, and be paid whenever it suits his convenience.

CHAPTER IV

COMMERCIAL ARBITRATION—ADJUSTMENT BUREAUS—COLLECTION AGENCIES

There are many instances where a controversy can be arbitrated more satisfactorily to both parties than the same controversy can be litigated. The processes of litigation are long and tedious and are very expensive as a rule. In some sections where court calendars are crowded a trial may not be reached for several years. Furthermore, in a law suit the issue is disposed of by strict technical legal procedure and strictly technical legal reasoning. How much more satisfactory it would be in many cases if a credit man or collector would enter into an arbitration agreement with a person or corporation with whom a controversy exists.

Each party selects some competent business man of sound judgment, or some reputable lawyer in high standing if the problem involved is thoroughly legal, and if the two arbitrators cannot agree they select a third, called the umpire; then they hold a meeting, procure the evidence in an orderly yet expeditious manner, and decide the equities of the situation from a good, commonsense standpoint. A decision of the two is final. Compare this method with the method of litigating these same matters, out of which litigation much bitterness grows and often counterclaims for damages are set up that the customer of the house never really intended to rely upon until urged to do so by some attorney seeking to set up a defense either for the purpose of gaining time or for the purpose of obtaining a more reasonable settlement—and frequently this counterclaim is set up without any real regard as to what is right or what is wrong.

Of course, there is some danger that the agreement to arbitrate might not be accepted as final by one faction or the other in case the verdict is not satisfactory, and in some states this might lead eventually to litigation if it is definitely established as the law of that state that an agreement to arbitrate is not binding. However, a carefully worded agreement to arbitrate, with an agreement recited therein that a judgment may be entered based upon the findings of the arbitrators, fully setting up the rights of the parties, the methods of procedure and other necessary details, is rarely ever disturbed by either party, even though it might not be legally binding. It would require a gross miscarriage of justice, or fraud upon the part of the arbitrators, to render a verdict so unsatisfactory as to result in litigating the same question, after it had been fairly arbitrated.

Therefore, the collector or credit man, when he realizes a controversy cannot be settled by a heart to heart talk or by the usual methods, should, when placing the matter in the hands of an attorney, recommend that the attorney negotiate an arbitration agreement, if possible and consistent. This suggestion is made for the reason that very few lawyers recommend a settlement by arbitration, as their usual habits, procedure and training is that disputes are settled by the courts and that that is what the courts are ordained for. But much time, expense and vexation can be saved by arbitration agreements, when compared to law suits.

In the February, 1919, issue of the Official Bulletin of the Chicago Association of Credit Men, page 20, the following interesting reference is made to Commercial Arbitration:

"The Chicago Association of Commerce has now taken up the subject in earnest; has appointed a committee of ten to have general charge of association organization on commercial arbitration; is appointing arbitration committees of three in each of their fifty-four trade subdivisions; will assign a secretary at Association headquarters to head up the work there, receive requests for and arrange for arbitrations; a sub-committee is working out compact and practical rules for conducting arbitrations; a publicity sub-committee has been appointed; and it is evident that the Association of Commerce members are not only to be fully informed of the many advantages to be derived from settling disputes out of court by arbitration, but it is to be made easy and practical for them to do so.

"Credit men should surely be among the first to recognize and make use of this modern procedure. They should acquaint their purchasing agents with the facilities now made available by the Association of Commerce. They should seriously undertake to incorporate in their contracts, and in their applications for credit and in property statement forms, a clause similar to the following:

"'Any dispute that may arise out of the purchase of goods under this contract, which the parties in interest may be unable to settle between themselves, shall be referred to arbitration under the laws of the State of Illinois and the rules of the Arbitration Bureau of the Chicago Association of Commerce.'"

" Credit men and purchasing agents and sales managers should cultivate the habit of always considering the possibility of settling a dispute by arbitration, before resorting to the law. No rights are jeopardized— a judgment may, if deemed desirable, be entered on an award; also an appeal may be taken. London has 100,000 arbitrations per year and with all its vast commerce gets along with comparatively few judges, juries, courts and civil cases. Why not Chicago? The answer lies with each individual one of us."

The affairs of many involved debtors are liquidated through adjustment bureaus of the various associations of credit men, and at the New York meeting of the National Association of Credit Men held in 1906 a committee on adjustment bureaus which had been appointed a year previous, according to the bulletin of the National Association of Credit Men of July, 1906, outlined the fundamental aims and objects of adjustment bureaus as follows:

(1) "To investigate upon request the affairs of a debtor reported to be insolvent and adjust the estate, when possible, without court proceedings."

(2) "To secure capable and efficient receivers and appraisers, or trustees, when court proceedings are found to be necessary."

(3) "To secure quick adjustment of all honest failures at a minimum cost and with a maximum dividend to creditors."

(4) "To facilitate and economically secure extensions or liquidations when upon investigation it is found to be to the best interests of all."

(5) "To influence concerted action by the creditors for the benefit of all."

(6) "To assist creditors to acquire for their own use the estate of failing or insolvent debtors, when mutually agreed upon."

(7) "To prosecute or assist in the prosecution of the guilty party or parties where investigation discloses fraud or the attempt to defraud."

This statement of the aims and objects of adjustment

bureaus is quite complete, and from such statements it will be seen that adjustment bureaus undertake to get concerted action on the part of creditors and to prevent friends of the debtor from being appointed as receivers, appraisers or trustees; to prevent the dissipation of assets that usually occurs in bankruptcy proceedings; the elimination of excessive attorneys' fees; and the prosecution of fraudulent debtors—in short, the adjustment bureaus attempt to undertake to liquidate an estate just as an estate is liquidated in bankruptcy, but to do so by more competent administration in a more expeditious manner at a lower expense, with the additional advantage of arranging an extension to worthy and honest debtors who with such an extension can probably work out their affairs, pay their creditors in full and preserve their business.

It is usually common practice now for a member of the National Association of Credit Men to notify the secretary of the adjustment bureau in his district that a certain debtor should be investigated and this results in calling a meeting of the creditors of the person reported. A committee of creditors is then appointed, usually with power to act, and foreign creditors are notified. An accurate statement of the financial condition of the debtor is secured and an inventory of the property. The committee of creditors then has full information and can act intelligently, and if circumstances warrant, an extension is granted; otherwise, a trustee is placed in charge, the debtor is required to make an assignment for the benefit of his creditors, and then, of course, if he refuses to do so, a bankruptcy petition is filed.

These adjustment bureaus usually have skilled appraisers and facilities for collecting accounts, and avenues through which stocks of merchandise can be disposed of to advantage. Ordinarily the charges of the bureau to its members do not exceed five or six per cent of the amount distributed to creditors, excepting for unusual services, though some associations charge a higher fee to nonmember creditors. These adjustment bureaus usually return to creditors from 55% to 60% of the amount of their claims, and this averages much higher than the return in bankruptcy cases, which we believe can fairly be stated to average not more than 25%.

If the reader of this book is a member of the National Association of Credit Men, he has already learned from experience the advantage of placing his claim with some adjustment bureau of the National Association of Credit Men, and from that experience has learned that the affairs of insolvent debtors are more promptly and more efficiently managed than would be the case in the average bankruptcy administration, and the returns he will have are far more satisfactory; if the reader is not a member of the National Association of Credit Men, he is urged to place claims against involved debtors with adjustment bureaus anyway rather than with attorneys who may undertake to throw the debtor into bankruptcy.

Just when to place an account for collection with a collection agency is a question that is often hard to determine. If the collection department waits too long the debtor is so involved that the loss is proportionately greater, and if the account is placed for collection too soon a collection agency will probably collect the account, but the debtor will get on his feet and be embittered and then the collection department is charged with driving away business from the firm.

In Chapter VI of this book there will be an outline of how you may organize and conduct your own collection agency, with practically no expense, and be in full possession all the time of the status of each claim. Practically the only expense involved will be that covering fees paid to attorneys, if a suit is necessary, and court costs. The operation of your own collection agency is not theoretical, but by actual practice in a large business it has proven to be a distinct advantage.

However, for the benefit of those who do not care to operate their own collection agency, attention is called to public collection agencies. Very many collection agencies are inefficient, and others are not trustworthy. Care should be taken in the selection of your collection agency. Often business is placed due to personal friendship without regard to efficiency, and after relations are once established claims keep going to the same collection concern without reference to the results accomplished, relying entirely upon their faith in that particular agency unless gross errors or dishonesty intervene. Credit men should keep a record of the cost of collecting accounts through this medium. The sales department figures the cost of getting business; the management, the per cent of expense; overhead is figured carefully; yet very few concerns keep any record of the percentage of cost on the year's business placed with the collection agencies.

If credit is extended with a reasonable amount of judgment, and the claim is placed at the proper time with the collection agency and the collection agency is efficient and honest, 75% of the business placed with them should result in full collection. The older an account becomes the harder it is to collect, but if you do not wait too long before placing business with a collection agency many of your doubtful claims should be recovered.

It is a good plan to call for the original letters received by the collection agency from debtors once in a while to see if they are reporting the facts as they exist and that you are not being misled. It is well to remember, too, that for the ordinary collection claim a collection agency is better organized to handle it than attorneys are. Attorneys can attend to legal procedure, but very few of them are equipped to handle detail collection work.

Sometimes collection agencies are blamed for failure to get results when they are not wholly to blame, due to carelessness on the part of the credit or collection department. Fundamentally the collection of an account begins when credit is first extended, for that is when the foundation is first laid for collecting the account. It is recommended that as soon as it has been determined that an account needs special attention, or when excuses for non-payment are not satisfactory, that a further inquiry be made into the debtor's standing at that time; then when the claim is placed with the collection agency they should be given the benefit of all the information you have, as this will place them in a position to handle the account intelligently and to advantage. Sending a plain statement showing the balance due does not give the collection agency anything to work on, but if you send a full and complete statement showing the date of each purchase and all credits, and all correspondence, and all facts relating to a dispute, if there is a dispute, the collection agency has facts before them which will enable them to know how to deal with the account.

Referring again to the time when accounts should be placed for collection, it should be remembered that it is not wise to be hasty in seeking the aid of collection agencies merely to get rid of the burden of trying to persuade a customer who is unable or unwilling to pay, and yet too much delay may involve loss. Many solvent debtors are merely indifferent and negligent, but if you have used all approved methods, and there is a question about the solvency of the debtor, you should either undertake to collect through your own collection agency, as outlined in Part III, or place the account with some public collection agency for prompt attention, which can give nearly as good service and in whom you have almost as much confidence as you would in a collection agency operated by yourself.

CHAPTER V

BANKRUPTCY

Every collector should be familiar with the operation of the bankruptcy law,—not necessarily with all the technical procedure of the bankruptcy court, nor with the legal problems involved in contested matters, but he should be especially interested in the practical operation of the law, its purposes, how it is applied and some of the effects of its application.

The bankruptcy law is founded upon the equitable maxim that "equity is equality" and upon the principle of expediency and the highest regard for the greatest number. The whole theory of the bankruptcy law is that each creditor of the unfortunate bankrupt shall share alike rather than that some one creditor or class of creditors will have an advantage over another creditor or class of creditors. Of course, the creditors of the bankrupt are classified particularly as between those who are secured and those who are unsecured, and it should be the supreme effort of every collector to be in the secured class if bankruptcy intervenes.

There has been a great deal of criticism on the part of some as to the operation of the bankruptcy law, but it would seem that much of this criticism is due partly to the fact that creditors take very little interest in the bankrupt's affairs after the petition is filed. They all seem to think that matters will run along themselves, and as long as every one is to share and share alike no particular attention is paid to the administration of the estate by the creditors, and it is to endeavor to correct this mistaken practice that this chapter is largely directed.

In many instances the effects of the bankruptcy court are disappointing and this is felt more keenly by the creditor, because after having had his confidence in the debtor shaken by reason of the debtor's failure himself, he is doubly disappointed in having had his confidence in the bankruptcy court apparently misplaced when judged by the results in the administration of that particular estate. Often the creditor hopes to receive a large dividend and expects complete redress in the bankruptcy court, and frequently having reason to believe there has been fraud practiced concludes that the debtor will be sent to the penitentiary. Very often if the debtor should be subjected to some criminal penalty the very creditors who could furnish the evidence do not show enough interest in the case to produce the proper evidence.

That there are abuses of the bankruptcy law there can be no question, but its passage has certainly taken away the fear of fraudulent transfers and bills of sale and "midnight mortgages." Any of these fraudulent moves can be set aside by the operation of the bankruptcy laws by an involuntary petition if acted upon within the time prescribed. Since the passage of the law there can be no more pell-mell attachments, fraudulent conveyances, preferential transfers, favored receiverships, assignments, executions or chattel mortgages that are designed to benefit some creditors at the expense of others, or to benefit the debtor at the expense of his creditors at large.

The bankruptcy law is a credit man's law and its primary object is the equal distribution of the assets of the bankrupt. The law when first enacted, immediately after the Civil War, was primarily to discharge any honest and deserving citizens from a burden of debt which they could never hope to overcome under ordinary conditions, but the law of 1898, now in force, is built upon a solid foundation, and has for its purpose the advancement of commerce and the encouragement of trade through reasonable, honest venture.

Occasionally we hear of the whole law being condemned because of some individual case that was improperly handled, or through which there disappeared much of the assets. It seems to be a trait of human nature to condemn and to affect a superior disdain for subjects which are mysterious or shrouded in darkness, and, frankly, it is the author's belief that much of the opposition to the bankruptcy law among credit men and lawyers is the general lack of information as to the provisions of the law, the procedure to be followed and the part that the creditor must play in the affairs of the bankrupt at certain times during the administration of the estate.

The average case works out about like this. Some collection agency or attorney writes or telegraphs to the firm a communication which is referred to the collection department or to the credit man, stating that a certain concern has just filed a petition in bankruptcy, or that one is just about to be filed, either voluntary or involuntary. This letter usually intimates that the informant has some first information and that instant action is necessary and the impulse is to promptly accept the invitation and send the requisite authority to a stranger or to one whose motives are wholly unknown to the creditor and whose integrity or policy of doing business is likewise unknown to the creditor.

There is no reason in the world why it is necessary to respond to these requests promptly. The collector or credit man has ample opportunity to fully investigate the case, as there is no advantage gained by filing a claim promptly or by delegating a power of attorney to one who has not been investigated, for the reason that it will be at least thirty days before even the first meeting of creditors can be held to elect a trustee. It is desirable, of course, for a creditor to file his claim so that he may vote for a trustee and in that way join with the other creditors in electing a trustee who is competent to administer the estate, and not some attorney or other person who will let it administer itself, knowing that his fees will be practically the same in either case. Furthermore a creditor has a year after the date of bankruptcy within which to present his claim for proof and allowance.

Therefore, go a little slow and when you are solicited to turn your claim over make the same investigation that you would in case you were extending credit, for remember that most of these solicitations are either for the purpose of getting fees from distant creditors, or some concern is being hustled through bankruptcy with some trustee in control who may represent interests that expect to acquire the estate, cheap, in toto.

Many estates also are not properly administered, for the reason that some creditors who do attend the first meeting of creditors have so little information as to bankruptcy procedure that their vote is cast out. The writer has attended the first meetings of creditors and has seen a large number of claims thrown out so far as a vote for the trustee is concerned because their claim was not in provable shape. At the first meeting of the creditors the referee calls for the proofs of claims of creditors attending in person or by attorney. This call results in the creditors stepping forward, but the attorneys are usually in the foreground and present bundles of claims which they have solicited and in proper order they are examined by the referee and are allowed. The creditors usually timidly move up and hand over a statement of their claim, or a copy of a note, or some other form of claim, not presented in provable shape and not sworn to, and they are then instructed by the referee to procure proper blanks, fill out their claim and swear to it. They usually step into another room and while there attempt to make out their claim, but before they can locate a notary and get the claim in fileable shape the election of the trustee is concluded. In that case the trustee is generally elected by the vote of claimants represented by attorneys.

The trustee employs his attorney, and usually employs the one who has worked the hardest in securing claims for his election, so that we can see that frequently the lack of knowing how to proceed in bankruptcy matters makes the bankruptcy court more or less of a political organization and makes it largely a lawyers' court instead of a creditors' court.

The writer believes too, that it is a great mistake to elect some model citizen as a trustee, or some man who has conducted a competitive business, in a belief that if he has made a success of his own business he can conduct the bankrupt's estate in such a way as to make it a success and pay a large dividend, with the ultimate possibility of paying out in full. If the bankrupt himself is honest, with his intimate knowledge of that particular business, his personal pride, the asset of his acquaintance, his knowledge of the customers of the business, their peculiarities, credit standing, habits of pay,—such a bankrupt himself is ordinarily the most competent man of all to operate that business with profit. Yet he has failed. How can the creditors expect to elect a stranger, with a business of his own to look after, who will give the bankrupt estate only an occasional smattering of time, to make a success of this business; he has his own interests and his own troubles, and the result is that due to lack of attention what few assets are left are dissipated; furthermore, it may not be to his advantage to successfully administer the estate of a competitor.

It should be remembered that the business of a trustee is not to operate a bankrupt estate but to liquidate and distribute. It is his business to sell the business or the assets, whatever they may be, and distribute the proceeds. Therefore, creditors should elect as trustee, if possible, one who does not have other interests absorbing their time, one who has not been a competitor of the bankrupt, but one who is tenacious, energetic and faithful.

Another important phase of the practical operation of the bankruptcy law with which credit men and collectors should be familiar is that dealing with preferences. Section 3, subdivision 2, of the Bankruptcy Act, states that acts of bankruptcy consist in having "transferred, while insolvent, any portion of his property to one or more of his creditors with intent to prefer such creditors over his other creditors."

Should a bankrupt commit an act of bankruptcy by attempting to prefer his creditors within this definition of a preference, proceedings to set aside such preference must be commenced within four months after said preference is created.

Section 60 of the Bankruptcy Act deals with preferred creditors, and Subdivision A is as follows:

"A person shall be deemed to have given a preference if, being insolvent, he has, within four months before the filing of the petition or after the filing of the petition and before the adjudication, procured or suffered a judgment to be entered against him in favor of any person, or made a transfer of any of his property, and the effect of the enforcement of such judgment or transfer will be to enable any one of his creditors to obtain a greater percentage of his debt than any other of such creditors of the same class. Where the preference consists in a transfer, such period of four months shall not expire until four months after the date of the recording or registering of the transfer, if by law such recording or registering is required."

An analysis of these two sections of the Bankruptcy Act, dealing with preferences, will show that Section 3, Subdivision 2, of the Bankruptcy Act, deals with the conduct and state of mind of the bankrupt before failure, but as defined in Section 60, preferences are dealt with from the standpoint of the trustee after the bankruptcy petition has been filed; that is to say, this section largely determines whether a trustee can recover from some favored creditor the advantage gained by that creditor over the other creditors of the same class in receiving some preference from the bankrupt before the petition is filed or after it was filed and before the adjudication took place.

In Mr. Remington's text-book on the subject of bankruptcy he divides a preference into eight elements, each of which must be proven by an ample amount of evidence, and Mr. Remington's classification is outlined, and the reader is directed to Mr. Remington's text-book on the subject of bankruptcy for a more comprehensive study on the subject of bankruptcy.

(1) Money paid or property conveyed must have come from the assets of the bankrupt and must have depleted his estate.

(2) Money paid or property conveyed must have actually been applied for the benefit of a creditor of the bankrupt.

(3) The preference received by the bankrupt's creditor must apply to a preceding debt.

(4) The preference must have been the voluntary act of the debtor.

(5) The money paid or property conveyed must

actually have been applied, in part or in full, upon an existing debt.

(6) At the time of such payment or transfer the debtor must have then been insolvent.

(7) The payment or transfer must have been within four months preceding the institution of bankruptcy proceedings, and where the preference occurred by means of a written document, and by the law of the locality such document is required to be registered or recorded, such registering or recording must have taken place within four months prior to the institution of the bankruptcy proceedings.

(8) An advantage must have accrued to the creditor receiving the preference out of the transaction as against all other general creditors of the estate.

In actual practice it is very difficult indeed for a trustee to recover for the benefit of the general creditors the preference given by the bankrupt to some one favored creditor. Usually the evidence of the bankrupt himself and the favored creditor is about all that is procurable. The bankrupt in such a case is very likely to feel that inasmuch as he favored this creditor he may get some favor in return after his discharge, such as obtaining credit again to get on his feet after he has "played square" with this creditor, and the creditor being anxious to maintain his preference is not very likely to admit at the time of its receipt that he knew the debtor was insolvent. Many of the jurymen, too, in a contest of this kind will think that under the same circumstances they would do the same thing and that the creditor was lucky to get his money, and if the other creditors were asleep on the job it is their own fault and they ought to suffer.

There is confusion as to when the four months begin to run as to instruments that are by law required to be registered or recorded; for instance, in some districts it has been held that the four months' limitation in Section 60 of the Bankruptcy Act does not begin until the date the instrument is recorded; while in other sections it is held that the four months begins to run upon the execution and delivery of the document irrespective of when it is recorded.

The same rule applies to transfers or encumbrances of personal property, but usually as to personal property the four months' limitation does not commence to run until the document is recorded, except in the case of conditional sales contracts, in which case the four months begin to run from the time of the execution and delivery thereof if under the laws of the state where executed no registering or recording is required; and, on the other hand, where the law requires such conditional sales contracts to be registered or recorded, the four months' limitation starts to run at the time of the registering or recording. However, in some states it has been decided that a conditional sales contract, if recorded at any time, before the filing of a petition in bankruptcy, is good as against all general creditors, and that the filing of such a contract does not create a preference.

The United States Bankruptcy Law is set out in this volume complete immediately following Part II.

CHAPTER VI

YOUR OWN COLLECTION AGENCY
ORGANIZATION—COLLECTION LETTERS—METHODS

Organizing and running a collection agency of your own is not a hobby or a pet theory but a practical proposition. All that it is necessary to do is to adopt a trade style or incorporate a company and arrange a satisfactory address to which replies can be sent, preferably the office of your attorneys, and get a suitable letterhead printed in sufficient quantity, and then dictate letters to delinquents in your own office and mail the letters from there, just as you would in the ordinary course of business.

The advantage of this procedure is that you maintain control of the collection of your own claims; that you get better efficiency, for the reason that credit men as a rule are better collectors than the average collection agency clerk, and you get the same benefit that a public collection agency gets by virtue of their name and the fact that they are in the collection business for the one purpose of making collections. Furthermore, the work involved is no greater than following up a collection agency for reports and for money returns, as most public collection agencies must be periodically followed, and following them up is as much effort as it is to follow the collection of a claim direct with the debtor.

The only expense involved is the expense of incorporating and that is avoided if a trade style is adopted. It is recommended, however, that the business be incorporated, as this gives the collection agency a better standing in the eyes of the debtor, and enables you to state on your letterhead under what laws the concern is organized, and the stock can be issued to dummies to conceal the real identity of the corporation and the dummies can be required to endorse the stock in blank, so that the real owners have actual control of the business.

Articles of incorporation vary in different states, but a letter to the secretary of the state under whose laws it is determined to incorporate, with a request for printed forms, will usually result in getting the blanks required for the purpose. However, several forms of incorporation are shown herein for guidance. The form in the state of New York is as follows:

CERTIFICATE OF INCORPORATION

OF

UNIVERSAL ADJUSTMENT COMPANY

We, the undersigned, all being of full age, all of us being citizens of the United States, and at least one of us being a resident of the State of New York, desiring to form a corporation pursuant to the

Business Corporation Law of the State of New York, do hereby certify, that

1. The name of the proposed corporation is the Universal Adjustment Company.

2. The purposes for which it is formed are to buy and sell promissory notes, mortgages, trust deeds, open book accounts, conditional and other sales contracts, and other evidences of indebtedness, for its own account and not as broker, providing, however, that it shall not exercise the functions of a bank in discounting any commercial paper and shall not engage in the business of loaning money, and also to conduct a general collection agency business.

3. The amount of the capital stock is $3,000.00.

4. The capital stock shall be divided into thirty shares of the par value of $100.00 each. The amount of capital with which said corporation shall begin business is $500.00.

5. The location of the principal business office is to be in the Borough of Manhattan, City of New York, State of New York.

6. The duration of the corporation is to be perpetual.

7. The number of its directors shall be three.

8. The names and post office addresses of the directors for the first year are as follows:

....

      (Name)   *(Post Office Address)*

....
....

9. The names and post office addresses of the subscribers, and the number of shares of stock which each agrees to take in the corporation, are as follows:

....

    (Name)   *(Post Office Address)*   *(Number of Shares)*

....
....

IN WITNESS WHEREOF, we have made and signed this certificate in duplicate this..............day of............, 19...
In presence of:

....
....
....
....
....

State of New York }
County of New York } ss.

On this..............day of.............., 19.., before me personally came.............., ..., ...,
to me personally known and known to me to be the individuals described in and who executed the foregoing instrument, and severally acknowledged that they executed the same for the uses and purposes therein mentioned.

....
(*Notary Public*)

The following form is the form for the State of Indiana:

ARTICLES OF ASSOCIATION

OF

UNIVERSAL ADJUSTMENT COMPANY

We, the undersigned, hereby associate ourselves together, pursuant to the statutes of the State of Indiana, for the organization of corporations, by the following written articles:

1. Name. The name shall be the Universal Adjustment Company.

2. Object. The object of this Association and the proposed plan for the transaction of its business shall be to buy and sell promis-

sory notes, mortgages, trust deeds and open book accounts, conditional and other sales contracts, and other evidences of indebtedness, for its own account and not as broker, providing, however, that it shall not exercise the functions of a bank in discounting any commerical paper and shall not engage in the business of loaning money, and also to conduct a general collection agency business.

3. The capital stock of this Association shall be $3,000.00, divided into thirty shares of $100.00 each.

4. Term of existence. The Association shall have an existence of twenty (not to exceed fifty) years from the date hereof.

5. Board of directors. There shall be three directors for this corporation, who after the first of the year shall be elected annually by the stockholders. All the corporate officers shall be appointed by the directors.

6. Place of operations. The business of this corporation shall be carried on in Indianapolis.

7. Directors for first year. The following directors shall manage the affairs and prudential concerns of this corporation for the first year of its existence.

....
....
....

IN WITNESS WHEREOF, we have hereunto set our hands this................................day of..............., 19...

(NOTE: The subscribers affix, in addition to their names, their residence, and, if a stock corporation, the number of shares taken by each.)

It is advisable to select a suitable name, such as The National Discount Company, The National Collection Company, The Universal Adjustment Company, or something similar. Although a post office box can be rented and used as the official address of the company, the better plan is to use the address of your attorneys, with their consent, as the official address of the company. Your attorneys will not object to this arrangement, and will arrange to daily re-forward or deliver to you all the mail received by them addressed to the collection agency.

The advantage of using the address of the attorneys is that if any debtor should call with the idea of making a personal visit to settle a claim, he will not find any connection between the concern to whom he is indebted and the collection agency.

If there are laws in the state requiring a collection agency to furnish a bond, or otherwise restrict them in any way that is unreasonable or undesirable, the claim can actually be sold to the collection agency by an assignment of the account, endorsement of a note, or a transfer of the obligation in any other form, so that they will appear as the actual bona fide holders of the claim.

It has been found advantageous to state on the letterhead that the company deals in stocks, bonds, mortgages, securities, and does a general collection business. If some debtor does call on your attorneys and desires to make settlement, he can then call for your file of papers and make some settlement, and you can pay him a reasonable fee for his services.

Should it be desired to avoid the expense of organizing a corporation, the adoption of a trade name will accomplish the same purpose, though there is more danger of having the relationship between the firm and the collection agency revealed, either through the filing of the articles of adoption of trade name or in some other way. However, as the fee for organizing corporations is usually a very nominal sum, that is by far the better plan of conducting your own collection agency.

In writing a debtor you have the advantage of knowing all about the past history of his relations with the firm and can better judge how he shall be approached than some public collection agency could who had no experience with him. At the same time collection agency letters can be very much more drastic than the letters which were previouly sent to this debtor under the firm name. The average public collection agency has a printed form which they send out notifying the debtor that they have a claim for collection and demanding immediate attention. Some of them in their printed notice threaten suit within a certain number of days. Operating your own collection agency gives you the same advantage that any other collection agency would have against the debtor, and gives you the additional advantage of knowing the customer and better determining from that how to proceed to enforce collection and enables you to maintain a direct control over such claims at the same time.

It is assumed that when a claim gets into the hands of some agency for collection there is no thought of attempting to retain the good will of the customer, and thus you may go the limit in making any kind of demand or threat that will most likely result in collection. However, if the nature of the debtor indicates that the use of suggestions may be adopted or persuasive methods pursued, that procedure may be followed, but ordinarily these tactics have already been tried out and it is questionable if they would be successful even though the added force of a collection agency is possible.

If the debtor actually fears a suit, he may accept a suggestion to pay the obligation in installments. If the debtor is known to have a certain amount of pride, or fears publicity, threatening to advertise the obligation for sale is sometimes effective. The notice of sale may be placed in the debtor's home newspaper, or a small printed poster be placed in front of his office or in front of his residence. If you know where he banks, he is frequently stirred up if the collection agency write to his bank offering to sell the claim to the bank at a discount, sending him a carbon copy of the letter. He will not know to what extreme you will go when he sees these methods being pursued, and if there is any way for him to get the money he will pay the claim, rather than be further harassed. Some debtors are aroused to action by sending a dun in a mourning envelope.

If all efforts to collect by mail have failed, the claim

should, of course, be placed in the hands of an attorney through your own collection agency. It is desirable to use a first-class attorney, whose name should be taken from some list of recommended attorneys, and if the credit man has a general knowledge of law, and a fair knowledge of the debtor's affairs, he can frequently make suggestions to attorneys as to how to proceed to collect; that is to say, he will know whether to threaten suit or actually commence suit, whether to attach certain property or whether the debtor should be threatened with a bankruptcy proceeding. In states where the law permits a judgment debtor to be examined, the attorney should be instructed to cite him for an examination under supplementary proceedings.

Where business is sent to lawyers by mail, the usual rule is for the attorney to retain two-thirds of the fee and send the correspondent (in this case your own collection agency) one-third of the fee, and if you will get your notes in such shape that attorney's fees are included your agency will not only operate at a sufficient profit to cover all the expenses of stationary, stamps, etc., but there may be some surplus to apply on your losses and bad accounts.

PART III
UNITED STATES BANKRUPTCY LAW

UNITED STATES BANKRUPTCY LAW

COMPLETE
INCLUDING AMENDMENTS OF 1910

An Act to Create a Uniform System of Bankruptcy in the United States and Territories

CHAPTER I

Definitions

1. Meaning of Words and Phrases.

CHAPTER II

Creation of Courts of Bankruptcy and their Jurisdiction

2. Courts and Jurisdiction.

CHAPTER III

Bankrupts

3. Acts of Bankruptcy.
4. Who may become Bankrupts.
5. Partners.
6. Exemption of Bankrupts.
7. Duties of Bankrupts.
8. Death or Insanity of Bankrupts.
9. Protection and Detention of Bankrupts.
10. Extradition of Bankrupts.
11. Suits by and against Bankrupts.
12. Compositions, when Confirmed.
13. Compositions, when Set Aside.
14. Discharges, when Granted.
15. Discharges, when Revoked.

16. Co-debtors of Bankrupts.
17. Debts not Affected by Discharge.

CHAPTER IV

Courts and Procedure Therein

18. Process, Pleadings, and Adjudications.
19. Jury Trials.
20. Oaths, Affirmations.
21. Evidence.
22. Reference of Cases after Adjudication.
23. Jurisdiction of United States and State Courts.
24. Jurisdiction of Appellate Courts.
25. Appeals and Writs of Error.
26. Arbitration of Controversies.
27. Compromises.
28. Designation of Newspapers.
29. Offenses.
30. Rules, Forms, and Orders.
31. Computation of Time.
32. Transfer of Cases.

CHAPTER V

Officers, their Duties and Compensation

33. Creation of Two Offices.
34. Appointment, Removal and Districts of Referees.
35. Qualifications of Referees.
36. Oath of Office of Referees.
37. Number of Referees.
38. Jurisdiction of Referees.
39. Duties of Referees.
40. Compensation of Referees.
41. Contempts before Referees.
42. Records of Referees.
43. Referee's Absence or Disability.
44. Appointment of Trustees.
45. Qualifications of Trustees.

46. Death or Removal of Trustees.
47. Duties of Trustees.
48. Compensation of Trustees.
49. Accounts and Papers of Trustees.
50. Bonds of Referees and Trustees.
51. Duties of Clerks.
52. Compensation of Clerks and Marshals.
53. Duties of Attorney General.
54. Statistics of Bankruptcy Proceedings.

CHAPTER VI

Creditors

55. Meetings of Creditors.
56. Voters at Meetings of Creditors.
57. Proof and Allowance of Claim.
58. Notice to Creditors.
59. Who may File and Dismiss Petitions.
60. Preferred Creditors.

CHAPTER VII

Estates

61. Depositories for Money.
62. Expenses of Administering Estates.
63. Debts which may be Proved.
64. Debts which have Priority.
65. Declarations and Payments of Dividends.
66. Unclaimed Dividends.
67. Liens.
68. Set-offs and Counterclaims.
69. Possession of Property.
70. Title to Property.
71. Clerks to Keep Indexes.
72. Extra Fees Forbidden.

CHAPTER I

DEFINITIONS

Meaning of Words and Phrases:
Section 1.—a. The words and phrases used in this act and in proceedings pursuant hereto shall, unless the same be inconsistent with the context, be construed as follows: (1) "A person against whom a petition has been filed" shall include a person who has filed a voluntary petition; (2) "adjudication" shall mean the date of the entry of a decree that the defendant in a bankruptcy proceeding is a bankrupt, or if such decree is appealed from, then the date when such decree is finally confirmed; (3) "Appellate Courts" shall include the Circuit Courts of Appeals of the United States, the Supreme Courts of the Territories, and the Supreme Court of the United States; (4) "bankrupt" shall include a person against whom an involuntary petition or an application to set a composition aside or to revoke a discharge has been filed or who has filed a voluntary petition or who has been adjudged a bankrupt; (5) "clerk" shall mean the clerk of a court of bankruptcy; (6) "corporations" shall mean all bodies having any of the powers and privileges of private corporations not possessed by individuals or partnerships, and shall include

limited or other partnership associations organized under laws making the capital subscribed alone responsible for the debts of the association; (7) "court" shall mean the court of bankruptcy in which the proceedings are pending, and may include the referee; (8) "courts of bankruptcy" shall include the district courts of the United States and of the Territories, the Supreme Court of the District of Columbia, and the United States Court of Alaska; (9) "creditor" shall include any one who owns a demand or claim provable in bankruptcy, and may include his duly authorized agent, attorney or proxy; (10) "date of bankruptcy" or "time of bankruptcy," or "commencement of proceedings", or "bankruptcy" with reference to time, shall mean the date when the petition was filed; (11) "debt" shall include any debt, demand or claim provable in bankruptcy; (12) "discharge" shall mean the release of a bankrupt from all of his debts which are provable in bankruptcy, except such as are excepted by this act; (13) "document" shall include any book, deed or instrument in writing; (14) "holiday" shall include Christmas, the Fourth of July, the Twenty-second of February and any day appointed by the President of the United States or the Congress of the United States as a holiday or as a day of public fasting or thanksgiving; (15) a person shall be deemed insolvent within the provisions of this act whenever the aggregate of his property, exclusive of any property which he may have conveyed,

DEFINITIONS

transferred, concealed or removed, with intent to defraud, hinder or delay his creditors, shall not at a fair valuation be sufficient in amount to pay his debts; (16) "judge" shall mean a judge of a court of bankruptcy, not including the referee; (17) "oath" shall include affirmation; (18) "officer" shall include clerk, marshal, receiver, referee and trustee, and the imposing of a duty upon or the forbidding of an act by any officer shall include his successor and any person authorized by law to perform the duties of such officer; (19) "persons" shall include corporations, except where otherwise specified, and officers, partnerships, and women, when used with reference to the commission of acts which are herein forbidden, shall include persons who are participants in the forbidden acts, and the agents, officers, and members of the board of directors or trustees, or other similar controlling bodies of corporations; (20) "petition" shall mean a paper filed in a court of bankruptcy or with a clerk or deputy clerk by a debtor praying for the benfits of this act, or by creditors alleging the commission of an act of bankruptcy, by a debtor therein named; (21) "referee" shall mean the referee who has jurisdiction of the case or to whom the case has been referred, or any one acting in his stead, (22) "conceal" shall include secrete, falsify and mutilate; (23) "secured creditor" shall include a creditor who has security for his debt upon the property of the bankrupt of a nature to be assignable under this act, or who owns such a debt for which some indorser, surety, or other persons secondarily liable for the bankrupt has such security upon the bankrupt's assets; (24) "States" shall include the Territories, Alaska, and the District of Columbia; (25) "transfer" shall include the sale and every other and different mode of disposing of or parting with property, or the possession of property absolutely or conditionally, as a payment, pledge, mortgage, gift or security; (26) "trustee" shall include all of the trustees of an estate; (27) "wage-earner" shall mean an individual who works for wages, salary, or hire, at a rate of compensation not exceeding one thousand five hundred dollars per year; (28) words importing the masculine gender may be applied to and include corporations, partnerships, and women; (29) words importing the plural number may be applied to and mean only a single person or thing; (30) words importing the singular number may be applied to and mean several persons or things.

CHAPTER II

CREATION OF COURTS OF BANKRUPTCY AND THEIR JURISDICTION

Courts and Jurisdiction:

Sec. 2. That the courts of bankruptcy as hereinbefore defined, viz.: the district courts of the United States in the several States, the Supreme Court of the District of Columbia, the district courts of the several Territories, and the United States courts in the District of Alaska, are hereby made courts of bankruptcy, and are hereby invested, within their respective territorial limits as now established, or as they may be hereafter changed, with such jurisdiction at law and in equity as will enable them to exercise original jurisdiction in bankruptcy proceedings, in vacation in chambers and during their respective terms, as they are now or may be hereafter held, to (1) adjudge persons bankrupt who have had their principal place of business, resided, or had their domicile within their respective territorial jurisdictions for the preceding six months, or the greater portion thereof, or who do not have their principal place of business, reside, or have their domicile within the United States, but have property within their jurisdiction, or who have been adjudged bankrupts by courts of competent jurisdiction without the United States, and have property within their jurisdiction; (2) allow claims, disallow claims, reconsider allowed or disallowed claims, and allow or disallow them against bankrupt estates; (3) appoint receivers or the marshal upon application of parties in interest in case the court shall find it absolutely necessary, for the preservation of estates, to take charge of the property of bankrupts after the filing of the petition and until it is dismissed or the trustee is qualified; (4) arraign, try, and punish bankrupts, officers, and other persons, and the agents, officers, members of the board of directors or other similar controlling bodies of corporations for violation of this act, in accordance with the laws of procedure of the United States now in force, or such as may be hereafter enacted, regulating trials for the alleged violation of laws of the United States; (5) authorize the business of bankrupts to be conducted for limited periods by receivers, the marshals, or trustees, if necessary in the best interests of the estates, and allow such officers additional compensation for such services, as provided in section forty-eight of this act; (6) bring in and substitute additional persons or parties in proceedings of bankruptcy when necessary for the complete determination of a matter in controversy; (7) cause the estates of bankrupts to be collected, reduced to money and distributed and determine controversies in relation thereto, except as herein otherwise provided; (8) close estates whenever it appears that they have been fully administered, by approving the final accounts and discharging the trustees, and reopen them whenever it appears they were closed before being fully administered; (9) confirm or reject compositions between debtors and their creditors, and set aside compositions and reinstate the cases; (10) consider and confirm, modify or overrule, or return, with instructions for further proceedings, records and findings certified to them by referees; (11) determine all claims of bankrupts to their exemptions; (12) discharge or refuse to discharge bankrupts and set aside discharge and reinstate the cases; (13) enforce obedience by bankrupts, officers, and other persons to all lawful orders, by fine or imprisonment or fine and imprisonment; (14) extradite bankrupts from their respective districts to other districts; (15) make such orders, issue such process, and enter such judgments in addition to those specifically provided for as may be necessary for the enforcement of the provisions of this Act; (16) punish persons for contempts committed before referees; (17) pursuant to the recommendation of creditors, or when they neglect to recommend the appointment of trustees, appoint trustees, and upon complaints of creditors, remove trustees for cause upon hearings and after notices to them; (18) tax costs, whenever they are allowed by law, and render judgments therefor against the unsuccessful party, or the successful party for cause, or in part against each of the parties, and against estates, in proceedings in bankruptcy; and (19) transfer cases to other courts of bankruptcy, and (20) exercise ancillary jurisdiction over persons or property within their respective territorial limits in aid of a receiver or trustee appointed in any bankruptcy proceedings pending in any other court of bankruptcy.

Nothing in this section contained shall be construed to deprive a court of bankruptcy of any power it would possess were certain specific powers not herein enumerated.

CHAPTER III

BANKRUPTS

Acts of Bankruptcy:

Sec. 3.—a. Acts of bankruptcy by a person shall consist of his having (1) conveyed, transferred, concealed, or removed, or permitted to be concealed or removed, any part of his property with intent to hinder, delay, or defraud his creditors, or any of them; or (2) transferred, while insolvent, any portion of his property to one or more of his creditors with intent to prefer such creditors over his other creditors; or (3) suffered or permitted, while insolvent, any creditor to obtain a preference through legal proceedings, and not having at least five days before a sale or final disposition of any property affected by such preference vacated or discharged such preference; or (4) made a general assignment for the benefit of his creditors or, being insolvent, applied for a receiver or trustee for his property or because of insolvency a receiver or trustee has been put in charge of his property under the laws of a State, of a Territory, or of the United States; or (5) admitted in writing his inability to pay his debts and his willingness to be adjudged a bankrupt on that ground.

b. A petition may be filed against a person who is insolvent and who has committed an act of bankruptcy within four months after the omission of such act. Such time shall not expire until four months after (1) the date of the recording or registering of the transfer or assignment when the act consists in having made a transfer of any of his property with intent to hinder, delay, or defraud his creditors or for the purpose of giving a preference as hereinbefore provided, or a general assignment for the benefit of his creditors, if by law such recording or registering is required or permitted, or, if it is not, from the date when the beneficiary takes notorious, exclusive, or continuous possession of the property unless the petitioning creditors have received actual notice of such transfer or assignment.

c. It shall be a complete defense to any proceedings in bankruptcy instituted under the first subdivision of this section to allege and prove that the party proceeded against was not insolvent as defined in this Act at the time of the filing the petition against him, and if solvency at such date is proved by the alleged bankrupt the proceedings shall be dismissed, and under the said subdivision one the burden of proving solvency shall be on the alleged bankrupt.

d. Whenever a person against whom a petition has been filed as herein provided under the second and third subdivisions of this section takes issue with and denies the allegation of his insolvency, it shall be his duty to appear in court on the hearing, with his books, papers, and accounts, and submit to an examination, and give testimony as to all matters tending to establish solvency or insolvency, and in case of his failure to so attend and submit to examination the burden of proving his solvency shall rest upon him.

e. Whenever a petition is filed by any person for the purpose of having another adjudged a bankrupt, and an application is made to take charge of and hold the property of the alleged bankrupt, or any part of the same, prior to the adjudication and pending a hearing on the petition, the petitioner or applicant shall file in the same court a bond with at least two good and sufficient sureties who shall reside within the jurisdiction of said court, to be approved by the court or a judge thereof, in such sum as the court shall direct, conditional for the payment, in case such petition is dismissed, to the respondent, his or her personal representatives, all costs, expenses and damages occasioned by such seizure, taking, and detention of the property of the alleged bankrupt.

If such petition be dismissed by the court or withdrawn by the petitioner, the respondent, or respondents, shall be allowed all costs, counsel fees, expenses and damages occasioned by such seizure, taking or detention of such property. Counsel fees, costs, expenses, and damages shall be fixed and allowed by the court, and paid by the obligors in such bond.

Who may become Bankrupts:

Sec. 4.—a. Any person except a municipal, railroad, insurance, or banking corporation, shall be entitled to the benefits of this act as a voluntary bankrupt.

b. Any natural person, except a wage-earner, or a person engaged chiefly in farming or the tillage of the soil, any unincorporated company, and any moneyed, business, or commercial corporation, except a municipal, railroad, insurance or banking corporation, owing debts to the amount of one thousand dollars or over, may be adjudged an involuntary bankrupt upon default or an impartial trial, and shall be subject to the provisions and entitled to the benefits of this act.

The bankruptcy of a corporation shall not release its officers, directors, or stockholders, as such, from any liability under the laws of a State or Territory or of the United States.

Partners:

Sec. 5.—a. A partnership, during the continuation of the partnership business, or after its dissolution and before the final settlement thereof, may be adjudged a bankrupt.

b. The creditors of the partnership shall appoint the trustee; in other respects so far as possible the estate shall be administered as herein provided for other estates.

c. The court of bankruptcy which has jurisdiction

of one of the partners may have jurisdiction of all of the partners and of the administration of the partnership and individual property.

d. The trustee shall keep separate accounts of the partnership property and of the property belonging to the individual partners.

e. The expenses shall be paid from the partnership property and the individual property in such proportions as the court shall determine.

f. The net proceeds of the partnership property shall be appropriated to the payment of the partnership debts, and the net proceeds of the individual estate of each partner to the payment of his individual debts. Should any surplus remain of the property of any partner after paying his individual debts, such surplus shall be added to the partnership assets and be applied to the payment of the partnership debts. Should any surplus of the partnership property remain after paying the partnership debts, such surplus shall be added to the assets of the individual partners in the proportion of their respective interests in the partnership.

g. The court may permit the proof of the claim of the partnership estate against the individual estates, and vice versa, and may marshal the assets of the partnership estate and individual estates so as to prevent preferences and secure the equitable distribution of the property of the several estates.

h. In the event of one or more but not all of the

members of a partnership being adjudged bankrupt, the partnership property shall not be administered in bankruptcy, unless by consent of the partner or partners not adjudged bankrupt; but such partner or partners not adjudged bankrupt shall settle the partnership business as expeditiously as its nature will permit, and account for the interest of the partner or partners adjudged bankrupt.

Exemptions of Bankrupts:

Sec. 6.—a. This Act shall not affect the allowance to bankrupts of the exemptions which are prescribed by the State laws in force at the time of the filing of the petition in the State wherein they have had their domicile for the six months or the greater portion thereof immediately preceding the filing of the petition.

Duties of Bankrupts:

Sec. 7.—a. The bankrupt shall (1) attend the first meeting of his creditors, if directed by the court or a judge thereof to do so, and the hearing upon his application for a discharge, if filed; (2) comply with all lawful orders of the court; (3) examine the correctness of all proofs of claims filed against his estate; (4) execute and deliver such papers as shall be ordered by the court; (5) execute to his trustee transfers of all his property in foreign countries; (6) immediately inform his trustee of any attempt, by his creditors, or other persons, to evade the provisions of this Act, coming to his knowledge; (7) in case of any person having to his knowledge proved a false claim against his estate, disclose that fact immediately to his trustee; (8) prepare, make oath to, and file in court within ten days, unless further time is granted, after the adjudication, if an involuntary bankrupt, and with the petition if a voluntary bankrupt, a schedule of his property, showing the amount and kind of property, the location thereof, its money value in detail, and a list of his creditors, showing their residences, if unknown, that fact to be stated, the amounts due each of them, the consideration thereof, the security held by them, if any, and a claim for such exemptions as he may be entitled to, all in triplicate, one copy of each for the clerk, one for the referee, and one for the trustee; and (9) when present at the first meeting of his creditors, and at such other times as the court shall order, submit to an examination concerning the conducting of his business, the cause of his bankruptcy, his dealings with his creditors, and other persons, the amount, kind, and whereabouts of his property, and, in addition, all matters which may affect the administration and settlement of his estate; but no testimony given by him shall be offered in evidence against him in any criminal proceeding.

Provided, however, that he shall not be required to attend a meeting of his creditors, or at or for an examination at a place more than one hundred and fifty miles distant from his home or principal place of business, or to examine claims except when presented to him, unless ordered by the court, or a judge thereof, for cause shown, and the bankrupt shall be paid his actual expenses from the estate when examined or required to attend at any place other than the city, town or village of his residence.

Death or Insanity of Bankrupts:

Sec. 8.—a. The death or insanity of a bankrupt shall not abate the proceedings, but the same shall be conducted and concluded in the same manner, so far as possible, as though he had not died or become insane: Provided, that in case of death the widow and children shall be entitled to all rights of dower and allowance fixed by the laws of the State of the bankrupt's residence.

Protection and Detention of Bankrupts:

Sec. 9.—a. A bankrupt shall be exempt from arrest upon civil process except in the following cases: (1) When issued from a court of bankruptcy for contempt or disobedience of its lawful orders; (2) when issued from a State court having jurisdiction, and served within such State, upon a debt or claim from which his discharge in bankruptcy would not be a release, and in such case he shall be exempt from such arrest when in attendance upon a court of bankruptcy or engaged in the performance of a duty imposed by this Act.

b. The judge may, at any time after the filing of a

petition by or against a person, and before the expiration of one month after the qualification of the trustee, upon satisfactory proof by the affidavits of at least two persons that such bankrupt is about to leave the district in which he resides or has his principal place of business to avoid examination, and that his departure will defeat the proceedings in bankruptcy, issue a warrant to the marshal, directing him to bring such bankrupt forthwith before the court for examination. If upon hearing the evidence of the parties it shall appear to the court or a judge thereof that the allegations are true and that it is necessary, he shall order such marshal to keep such bankrupt in custody not exceeding ten days, but not imprison him, until he shall be examined and released or give bail conditioned for his appearance for examination, from time to time, not exceeding in all ten days, as required by the court, and for his obedience to all lawful orders made in reference thereto.

Extradition of Bankrupts:

Sec. 10.—a. Whenever a warrant for the apprehension of a bankrupt shall have been issued, and he shall have been found within the jurisdiction of a court other than the one issuing the warrant, he may be extradited in the same manner in which persons under indictment are now extradited from one district within which a district court has jurisdiction to another.

Suits By and Against Bankrupts:

Sec. 11.—a. A suit which is founded upon a claim from which a discharge would be a release, and which is pending against a person at the time of the filing of a petition against him, shall be stayed until after an adjudication or the dismissal of the petition; if such person is adjudged a bankrupt, such action may be further stayed until twelve months after the date of such adjudication, or, if within that time such person applies for a discharge, then until the question of such discharge is determined.

b. The court may order the trustee to enter his appearance and defend any pending suit against the bankrupt.

c. A trustee may, with the approval of the court, be permitted to prosecute as trustee any suit commenced by the bankrupt prior to the adjudication, with like force and effect as though it had been commenced by him.

d. Suits shall not be brought by or against a trustee of a bankrupt estate subsequent to two years after the estate has been closed.

Compositions, when Confirmed:

Sec. 12.—a. A bankrupt may offer, either before or after adjudication, terms of composition to his creditors after, but not before, he has been examined in open court or at a meeting of his creditors and has filed in court the schedule of his property and list of his creditors, required to be filed by bankrupts. In compositions before adjudication the bankrupt shall file the required schedules, and thereupon the court shall call a meeting of creditors for the allowance of claims, examination of the bankrupt, and preservation or conduct of estates, at which meeting the judge or referee shall preside, and action upon the petition for adjudication shall be delayed until it shall be determined whether such composition shall be confirmed.

b. An application for the confirmation of a composition may be filed in the court of bankruptcy after, but not before, it has been accepted in writing by a majority in number of all creditors whose claims have been allowed, which number must represent a majority in amount of such claims, and the consideration to be paid by the bankrupt to his creditors, and the money necessary to pay all debts which have priority and the cost of the proceedings, have been deposited in such place as shall be designated by the subject to the order of the judge.

c. A date and place, with reference to the convenience of the parties in interest, shall be fixed for the hearing upon each application for the confirmation of a composition, and such objections as may be made to its confirmation.

d. The judge shall confirm a composition if satisfied that (1) it is for the best interests of the creditors; (2)

the bankrupt has not been guilty of any of the acts or failed to perform any of the duties which would be a bar to his discharge; and (3) the offer and its acceptance are in good faith and have not been made or procured except as herein provided, or by any means, promises, or acts herein forbidden.

e. Upon the confirmation of a composition, the consideration shall be distributed as the judge shall direct, and the case dismissed. Whenever a composition is not confirmed, the estate shall be administered in bankruptcy as herein provided.

Compositions, when set Aside:

Sec. 13.—a. The judge may, upon the application of parties in interest filed at any time within six months after a composition has been confirmed, set the same aside and reinstate the case if it shall be made to appear upon a trial that fraud was practiced in the procuring of such composition, and that the knowledge thereof has come to the petitioners since the confirmation of such composition.

Discharges, when Granted:

Sec. 14.—a. Any person may, after the expiration of one month and within the next twelve months subsequent to being adjudged a bankrupt, file an application for a discharge in the court of bankruptcy in which the proceedings are pending; if it shall be made to appear to the judge that the bankrupt was unavoidably prevented from filing it within such time, it may be filed within but not after the expiration of the next six months.

b. The judge shall hear the application for a discharge, and such proofs and pleas as may be made in opposition thereto by the trustee or other parties in interest, at such time as will give the trustee or parties in interest a reasonable opportunity to be fully heard, and investigate the merits of the application and discharge the applicant unless he has (1) committed an offense punishable by imprisonment as herein provided; or (2) with intent to conceal his financial condition, destroyed, concealed, or failed to keep books of account or records from which such condition might be ascertained; or (3) obtained money or property on credit upon a materially false statement in writing made by him to any person or his representative for the purpose of obtaining credit from such person; (4) at any time subsequent to the first day of the four months immediately preceding the filing of the petition transferred removed, destroyed, or concealed any of his property with intent to hinder, delay or defraud his creditors; or (5) in voluntary proceedings been granted a discharge in bankruptcy within six years; or (6) in the course of the proceedings in bankruptcy refused to obey any lawful order of, or to answer any material question approved by the court: Provided, that a trustee shall not interpose objections to a bankrupt's discharge until he shall be authorized so to do at a meeting of creditors called for that purpose.

c. The confirmation of a composition shall discharge the bankrupt from his debts, other than those agreed to be paid by the terms of the composition and those not affected by a discharge.

Discharges, when Revoked:

Sec. 15.—a. The judge may, upon the application of parties in interest who have not been guilty of undue laches, filed at any time within one year after a discharge shall have been granted, revoke it upon a trial if it shall be made to appear that it was obtained through the fraud of the bankrupt, and that the knowledge of the fraud has come to the petitioners since the granting of the discharge, and that the actual facts did not warrant the discharge.

Co-Debtors of Bankrupts:

Sec. 16.—a. The liability of a person who is a co-debtor with or guarantor or in manner surety for, a bankrupt shall not be altered by the discharge of such bankrupt.

Debts not Affected by Discharge:

Sec. 17.—a. A discharge in bankruptcy shall release a bankrupt from all of his provable debts, except such as (1) are due as a tax levied by the United States, the State, county, district or municipality in which he resides; (2) are liabilities for obtaining property by false pretenses or false representations, or for willful and malicious injuries to the person or property of another, or for alimony due or to become due, or for maintenance or support of wife or child, or for seduction of an unmarried female, or for criminal conversation; (3) have not been duly scheduled in time for proof and allowance, with the name of the creditor if known to the bankrupt, unless such creditor had notice or actual knowledge of the proceedings in bankruptcy; or (4) were created by his fraud, embezzlement, misappropriation, or defalcation while acting as an officer or in any fiduciary capacity.

CHAPTER IV

COURTS AND PROCEDURE THEREIN

Process, Pleadings, and Adjudications:

Sec. 18.—a. Upon the filing of a petition for involuntary bankruptcy, service thereof, with a writ of subpœna, shall be made upon the person therein named as defendant in the same manner that service of such process is now had upon the commencement of a suit in equity in the courts of the United States, except that it shall be returnable within fifteen days, unless the judge shall for cause fix a longer time; but in case personal service can not be made, then notice shall be given by publication in the same manner and for the same time as provided by law for notice by publication in suits to enforce a legal or equitable lien in courts of the United States, except that, unless the judge shall otherwise direct, the order shall be published not more than once a week for two consecutive weeks, and the return day shall be ten days after the last publication unless the judge shall for cause fix a longer time.

b. The bankrupt, or any creditor, may appear and plead to the petition within five days after the return day, or within such further time as the court may allow.

c. All pleadings setting up matters of fact shall be verified under oath.

d. If the bankrupt, or any of his creditors, shall appear, within the time limited, and controvert the facts alleged in the petition, the judge shall determine, as soon as may be, the issues presented by the pleading, without the intervention of a jury, except in cases where a jury trial is given by this Act, and make the adjudication or dismiss the petition.

e. If on the last day within which pleadings may be filed none are filed by the bankrupt or any of his creditors, the judge shall on the next day, if present, or as soon thereafter as practicable, make the adjudication or dismiss the petition.

f. If the judge is absent from the district, or the division of the district in which the petition is pending, on the next day after the last day on which pleadings may be filed, and none have been filed by the bankrupt or any of his creditors, the clerk shall forthwith refer the case to the referee.

g. Upon the filing of a voluntary petition the judge shall hear the petition and make the adjudication or dismiss the petition. If the judge is absent from the district, or the division of the district in which the petition is filed, at the time of the filing, the clerk shall forthwith refer the case to the referee.

Jury Trials:

Sec. 19.—a. A person against whom an involuntary petition has been filed shall be entitled to have a trial by jury, in respect to the question of his insolvency, except as herein otherwise provided, and any act of bankruptcy alleged in such petition to have been committed, upon filing a written application therefor at or before the time within which an answer may be filed. If such application is not filed within such time, a trial by jury shall be deemed to have been waived.

b. If a jury is not in attendance upon the court, one may be specially summoned for the trial, or the case may be postponed, or, if the case is pending in one of the district courts within the jurisdiction of a circuit court of the United States, it may be certified for trial to the circuit court sitting at the same place, or by consent of parties when sitting at any other place in the same district, if such circuit court has or is to have a jury first in attendance.

c. The right to submit matters in controversy, or an alleged offense under this Act, to a jury shall be determined and enjoyed, except as provided by this Act, according to the United States laws now in force or such as may be hereafter enacted in relation to trials by jury.

Oaths, Affirmations:

Sec. 20.—a. Oaths required by this Act, except upon hearings in court, may be administered by (1) referees; (2) officers authorized to administer oaths in proceedings before the courts of the United States, or under the laws of the State where the same are to be taken; and (3) diplomatic or consular officers of the United States in any foreign country.

b. Any person conscientiously opposed to taking an oath may, in lieu thereof, affirm. Any person who shall affirm falsely shall be punished as for the making of a false oath.

Evidence:

Sec. 21.—a. A court of bankruptcy may, upon application of any officer, bankrupt, or creditor, by order require any designated person, including the bankrupt and his wife, to appear in court or before a referee or the judge of any State court, to be examined concerning the acts, conduct, or property of a bankrupt, whose estate is in process of administration under this Act: Provided, That the wife may be examined only touching business transacted by her or to which she is a party, and to determine the fact whether she has transacted or been a party to any business of the bankrupt.

b. The right to take depositions in proceedings under this Act shall be determined and enjoyed according to the United States laws now in force, or such as may be hereafter enacted relating to the taking of depositions, except as herein provided.

c. Notice of the taking of depositions shall be filed

with the referee in every case. When depositions are to be taken in opposition to the allowance of a claim notice shall also be served upon the claimant, and when in opposition to a discharge notice shall also be served upon the bankrupt.

d. Certified copies of proceedings before a referee, or of papers, when issued by the clerk or referee, shall be admitted as evidence with like force and effect as certified copies of the records of district courts of the United States are now or may hereafter be admitted as evidence.

e. A certified copy of the order approving the bond of a trustee shall constitute conclusive evidence of the vesting in him of the title to the property of the bankrupt, and if recorded shall impart the same notice that a deed from the bankrupt to the trustee if recorded would have imparted had not the bankruptcy proceedings intervened.

f. A certified copy of an order confirming or setting aside a composition, or granting or setting aside a discharge, not revoked, shall be evidence of the jurisdiction of the court, the regularity of the proceedings, and of the fact that that the order was made.

g. A certified copy of an order confirming a composition shall constitute evidence of the revesting of the title of his property in the bankrupt, and if recorded shall impart the same notice that a deed from the trustee to the bankrupt if recorded would impart.

Reference of Cases after Adjudication:

Sec. 22.—a. After a person has been adjudged a bankrupt the judge may cause the trustee to proceed with the administration of the estate, or refer it (1) generally to the referee or specially with only limited authority to act in the premises or to consider and report upon specified issues; or (2) to any referee within the territorial jurisdiction of the court, if the convenience of parties in interest will be served thereby, or for cause, or if the bankrupt does not do business, reside, or have his domicile in the district.

b. The judge may, at any time, for the convenience of parties or for cause, transfer a case from one referee to another.

Jurisdiction of United States and State Courts:

Sec. 23.—a. The United States circuit courts shall have jurisdiction of all controversies at law and in equity, as distinguished from proceedings in bankruptcy, between trustees as such and adverse claimants concerning the property acquired or claimed by the trustees, in the same manner and to the same extent only as though bankruptcy proceedings had not been instituted and such controversies had been between the bankrupts and such adverse claimants.

b. Suits by the trustees shall be brought or prosecuted in the courts where the bankrupt, whose estate is being administered by such trustee, might have brought or prosecuted them if proceedings in bankruptcy had not been instituted, unless by consent of the proposed defendant, except suits for the recovery of property under section sixty, subdivision b, and section sixty-seven, subdivision e; and section seventy, subdivision e.

c. The United States circuit court shall have concurrent jurisdiction with the courts of bankruptcy, within their respective territorial limits, of the offenses enumerated in this Act.

Jurisdiction of Appellate Courts:

Sec. 24.—a. The Supreme Court of the United States, the circuit courts of appeals of the United States, and the supreme courts of the Territories, in vacation in chambers and during their respective terms, as now or as they may be hereafter held, are hereby invested with appellate jurisdiction of controversies arising in bankruptcy proceedings from the courts of bankruptcy from which they have appellate jurisdiction in other cases. The Supreme Court of the United States shall exercise a like jurisdiction from courts of bankruptcy not within any organized circuit of the United States and from the supreme court of the District of Columbia.

b. The several circuit courts of appeal shall have jurisdiction in equity, either interlocutory or final, to superintend and revise in matter of law the proceedings of the several inferior courts of bankruptcy within their jurisdiction. Such power shall be exercised on due notice and petition by any party aggrieved.

Appeals and Writs of Error:
Sec. 25.—a. That appeals, as in equity cases, may be taken in bankruptcy proceedings from the courts of bankruptcy to the circuit court of appeals of the United States, and to the supreme court of the Territories, in the following cases, to-wit, (1) from a judgment adjudging or refusing to adjudge the defendant a bankrupt; (2) from a judgment granting or denying a discharge; and (3) from a judgment allowing or rejecting a debt or claim of five hundred dollars or over. Such appeal shall be taken within ten days after the judgment appealed from has been rendered, and may be heard and determined by the appellate court in term or vacation, as the case may be.

b. From any final decision of a court of appeals allowing or rejecting a claim under this Act, an appeal may be had under such rules and within such time as may be prescribed by the Supreme Court of the United States, in the following cases and no other:

1. Where the amount in controversy exceeds the sum of two thousand dollars, and the question involved is one which might have been taken on appeal or writ of error from the highest court of a State to the Supreme Court of the United States; or

2. Where some Justice of the Supreme Court of the United States shall certify that in his opinion the determination of the question or questions involved in the allowance or rejection of such claim is essential to a uniform construction of this Act throughout the United States.

c. Trustees shall not be required to give bond when they take appeals or sue out writs of error.

d. Controversies may be certified to the Supreme Court of the United States from other courts of the United States, and the former court may exercise jurisdiction thereof and issue writs of certiorari pursuant to the provisions of the United States laws now in force or such as may be hereafter enacted.

Arbitration of Controversies:

Sec. 26.—a. The trustee may, pursuant to the direction of the court, submit to arbitration any controversy arising in the settlement of the estate.

b. Three arbitrators shall be chosen by mutual consent, or one by the trustee, one by the other party to the controversy, and the third by the two so chosen, or if they fail to agree in five days after their appointment the court shall appoint the third arbitrator.

c. The written finding of the arbitrators, or a majority of them, as to the issues presented, may be filed in court and shall have like force and effect as the verdict of a jury.

Compromises:

Sec. 27.—a. The trustee may, with the approval of the court, compromise any controversy arising in the administration of the estate upon such terms as he may deem for the best interests of the estate.

Designation of Newspapers:

Sec. 28.—a. Courts of bankruptcy shall by order designate a newspaper published within their respective territorial districts, and in the county in which the bankrupt resides or the major part of his property is situated, in which notices required to be published by this Act and orders which the court may direct to be published shall be inserted. Any court may in a particular case, for the convenience of parties in interest, designate some additional newspaper in which notices and orders in such case shall be published.

Offenses:

Sec. 29.—a. A person shall be punished, by imprisonment for a period not to exceed five years, upon conviction of the offense of having knowingly and fraudulently appropriated to his own use, embezzled, spent, or unlawfully transferred any property or secreted or destroyed any document belonging to a bankrupt estate which came into his charge as trustee.

b. A person shall be punished, by imprisonment for a period not to exceed two years, upon conviction of the offense of having knowingly and fraudulently (1) concealed while a bankrupt, or after his discharge, from his trustee any of the property belonging to his estate in bankruptcy; or (2) made a false oath or account in, or in relation to, any proceeding in bankruptcy; (3) presented under oath any false claim for proof against the estate of a bankrupt, or used any such claim in composition personally or by agent, proxy, or attorney, or as agent, proxy, or attorney; or (4) received any material amount of property from a bankrupt after the filing of the petition, with intent to defeat this Act; or (5) extorted or attempted to extort any money or property from any person as a consideration for acting or forbearing to act in bankruptcy proceedings.

c. A person shall be punished by fine, not to exceed five hundred dollars, and forfeit his office, and the same shall thereupon become vacant, upon conviction of the offense of knowingly (1) acted as a referee in a case in which he is directly or indirectly interested; or (2) purchased, while a referee, directly or indirectly, any property of the estate in bankruptcy of which he is referee; or (3) refused, while a referee or trustee, to permit a reasonable opportunity for the inspection of the accounts relating to the affairs of, and the papers and records of, estates in his charge by parties in interest when directed by the court so to do.

d. A person shall not be prosecuted for any offense arising under this Act unless the indictment is found or the information is filed in court within one year after the commission of the offense.

Rules, Forms and Orders:

Sec. 30.—a. All necessary rules, forms, and orders as to procedure and for carrying this Act into force and effect shall be prescribed, and may be amended from time to time, by the Supreme Court of the United States.

Computation of Time:

Sec. 31.—a. Whenever time is enumerated by days in this Act, or in any proceeding in bankruptcy, the number of days shall be computed by excluding the first and including the last, unless the last fall on a Sunday or holiday, in which event the day last included shall be the next day thereafter which is not a Sunday or a legal holiday.

Transfer of Cases:

Sec. 32.—a. In the event petitions are filed against the same person, or against different members of a partnership, in different courts of bankruptcy each of which has jurisdiction, the cases shall be transferred, by order of the courts relinquishing jurisdiction, to and be consolidated by the one of such courts which can proceed with the same for the greatest convenience of parties in interest.

CHAPTER V

OFFICERS, THEIR DUTIES AND COMPENSATION

Creation of Two Offices:

Sec. 33.—a. The offices of referee and trustee are hereby created.

Appointment, Removal and Districts of Referees:

Sec. 34.—a. Courts of bankruptcy shall, within the territorial limits of which they respectively have jurisdiction, (1) appoint referees, each for a term of two years, and may, in their discretion, remove them because their services are not needed or for other cause; and (2) designate, and from time to time change, the limits of the districts of referees, so that each county, where the services of a referee are needed, may constitute at least one district.

Qualifications of Referees:

Sec. 35.—a. Individuals shall not be eligible to appointment as referees unless they are respectively (1) competent to perform the duties of that office; (2) not holding any office of profit or emolument under the laws of the United States or of any State other than commissioners of deeds, justices of the peace, masters in chancery, or notaries public; (3) not related by consanguinity or affinity, within the third degree as determined by the common law, to any of the judges of the courts of bankruptcy or circuit courts of the United States, or of the justices or judges of the appellate courts of the districts wherein they may be appointed; and (4) residents of, or have their offices in, the territorial districts for which they are to be appointed.

Oaths of Office of Referees:
Sec. 36.—a. Referees shall take the same oath of office as that prescribed for judges of United States courts.

Number of Referees:
Sec. 37.—a. Such number of referees shall be appointed as may be necessary to assist in expeditiously transacting the bankruptcy business pending in the various courts of bankruptcy.

Jurisdiction of Referees:
Sec. 38.—a. Referees respectively are hereby invested, subject always to a review by the judge, within the limits of their districts as established from time to time, with jurisdiction to (1) consider all petitions referred to them by the clerks and make the adjudications or dismiss the petitions; (2) exercise the powers vested in courts of bankruptcy for the administering of oaths to and the examination of persons as witnesses and for requiring the production of documents in proceedings before them, except the power of commitment;

(3) exercise the powers of the judge for the taking possession and releasing of the property of the bankrupt in the event of the issuance by the clerk of a certificate showing the absence of a judge from the judicial district, or the division of the district, or his sickness, or inability to act; (4) perform such part of the duties, except as to questions arising out of the applications of bankrupts for compositions or discharges, as are by this Act conferred on courts of bankruptcy and as shall be prescribed by rules or orders of the courts of bankruptcy of their respective districts, except as herein otherwise provided; and (5) upon the application of the trustee during the examination of the bankrupts, or other proceedings, authorize the employment of stenographers at the expense of the estates at a compensation not to exceed ten cents per folio for reporting and transcribing the proceedings.

Duties of Referees:

Sec. 39.—a. Referees shall (1) declare dividends and prepare and deliver to trustees dividend sheets showing the dividends declared and to whom payable; (2) examine all schedules of property and lists of creditors filed by bankrupts and cause such as are incomplete or defective to be amended; (3) furnish such information concerning the estates in process of administration before them as may be requested by the parties in interest; (4) give notices to creditors as herein provided; (5) make up records embodying the evidence, or the substance thereof, as agreed upon by the parties in contested matters arising before them, whenever requested to do so by either of the parties thereto, together with their findings therein, and transmit them to the judges; (6) prepare and file the schedules of property and lists of creditors required to be filed by the bankrupts, or cause the same to be done, when the bankrupts fail, refuse, or neglect to do so; (7) safely keep, perfect, and transmit to the clerks the records, herein required to be kept by them, when the cases are concluded; (8) transmit to the clerks such papers as may be on file before them whenever the same are needed in any proceedings in courts, and in like manner secure the return of such papers after they have been used, or, if it be impracticable to transmit the original papers, transmit certified copies thereof by mail; (9) upon application of any party in interest, preserve the evidence taken or the substance thereof as agreed upon by the parties before them when a stenographer is not in attendance; and (10) whenever their respective offices are in the same cities or towns where the courts of bankruptcy convene, call upon and receive from the clerks all papers filed in courts of bankruptcy which have been referred to them.

b. Referees shall not (1) act in cases in which they are directly or indirectly interested; (2) practice as attorneys and counselors at law in any bankruptcy proceedings; or (3) purchase, directly or indirectly, any property of an estate in bankruptcy.

Compensation of Referees:
Sec. 40.—a. Referees shall receive as full compensation for their services, payable after they are rendered, a fee of fifteen dollars deposited with the clerk at the time the petition is filed in each case, except when a fee is not required from a voluntary bankrupt, and twenty-five cents for every proof of claim filed for allowance, to be paid from the estate, if any, as a part of the cost of administration, and from estates which have been administered before them one per centum commissions on all moneys disbursed to creditors by the trustee, or one-half of one per centum on the amount to be paid to creditors upon the confirmation of a composition.

b. Whenever a case is transferred from one referee to another the judge shall determine the proportion in which the fee and commission therefor shall be divided between the referees.

c. In the event of the reference of a case being revoked before it is concluded and when the case is specially referred, the judge shall determine what part of the fee and commissions shall be paid to the referee.

Contempts before Referees:
Sec. 41.—a. A person shall not, in proceedings before a referee, (1) disobey or resist any lawful order,

process, or writ; (2) misbehave during a hearing or so near the place thereof as to obstruct the same; (3) neglect to produce, after having been ordered to do so, any pertinent document; or (4) refuse to appear after having been subpœnaed, or, upon appearing, refuse to take the oath as a witness, or, after having taken the oath, refuse to be examined according to law; Provided, That no person shall be required to attend as a witness before a referee at a place outside of the State of his residence, and more than one hundred miles from such place of residence, and only in case his lawful mileage and fee for one day's attendance shall be first paid or tendered to him.

b. The referee shall certify the facts to the judge, if any person shall do any of the things forbidden in this section. The judge shall, thereupon, in a summary manner, hear the evidence as to the acts complained of, and, if it is such as to warrant him in so doing, punish such person in the same manner and to the same extent as for a contempt committed before the court of bankruptcy, or commit such person upon the same conditions as if the doing of the forbidden act had occurred with reference to the process of, or in the presence of, the court.

Records of Referees:

Sec. 42.—a. The records of all proceedings in each case before a referee shall be kept as nearly as may be in the same manner as records are now kept in equity cases in circuit courts of the United States.

b. A record of the proceedings in each case shall be kept in a separate book or books, and shall, together with the papers on file, constitute the records of the case.

c. The book or books containing a record of the proceedings shall, when the case is conducted before the referee, be certified to by him, and, together with such papers as are on file before him, be transmitted to the court of bankruptcy and shall there remain as a part of the records of the court.

Referee's Absence or Disability:

Sec. 43.—a. Whenever the office of a referee is vacant, or its occupant is absent or disqualified to act, the judge may act, or may appoint another referee, or another referee holding an appointment under the same court may, by order of the judge, temporarily fill the vacancy.

Appointment of Trustees:

Sec. 44.—a. The creditors of a bankrupt estate shall, at their first meeting after the adjudication or after a vacancy has occurred in the office of trustee, or after an estate has been reopened, or after a composition has been set aside or a discharge revoked, or if there is a vacancy in the office of trustee, appoint one trustee or three trustees of such estate. If the creditors do not appoint a trustee or trustees as herein provided, the court shall do so.

Qualifications of Trustees:

Sec. 45.—a. Trustees may be (1) individuals who are respectively competent to perform the duties of that office, and reside or have an office in the judicial district within which they are appointed, or (2) corporations authorized by their charters or by law to act in such capacity and having an office in the judicial district within which they are appointed.

Death or Removal of Trustees:

Sec. 46.—a. The death or removal of a trustee shall not abate any suit or proceeding which he is prosecuting or defending at the time of his death or removal, but the same may be proceeded with or defended by his joint trustee or successor in the same manner as though the same had been commenced or was being defended by such joint trustee alone or by such successor.

Duties of Trustees:

Sec. 47.—a. Trustees shall respectively (1) account for and pay over to the estates under their control all interest received by them upon property of such estates; (2) collect and reduce to money the property of the estates for which they are trustees, under the direction of the court, and close up the estate as expeditiously as is compatible with the best interests of the parties in interest; and such trustees, as to all property in the custody or coming into the custody of the bankruptcy court, shall be deemed vested with all the rights, remedies, and powers of a creditor holding a lien by legal or equitable proceedings thereon and also as to all property not in the custody of the bankruptcy court, shall be deemed vested with all the rights, remedies, and powers of a judgment creditor holding an execution duly returned unsatisfied; (3) deposit all money received by them in one of the designated depositories; (4) disburse money only by check or draft on the depositories in which it has been deposited; (5) furnish such information concerning the estates of which they are trustees and their administration as may be requested by parties in interest; (6) keep regular accounts showing all amounts received and from what source and all amounts expended and on what accounts; (7) lay before the final meeting of the creditors detailed statements of the administration of the estates; (8) make final reports and file final accounts with the courts fifteen days before the days fixed for the final meetings of the creditors; (9) pay dividends within ten days after they are declared by the referees; (10) report to the courts, in writing, the condition of the estates and the amounts of money on hand, and such other details as may be required by the courts, within the first month after their appointment and every two months thereafter, unless otherwise ordered by the courts; and (11) set apart the bankrupt's exemptions and report the items and estimated value thereof to the court as soon as practicable after their appointment.

b. Whenever three trustees have been appointed for an estate, the concurrence of at least two of them shall be necessary to the validity of their every act concerning the administration of the estate.

c. The trustee shall, within thirty days after the adjudication, file a certified copy of the decree of adjudication in the office where conveyancs of real estate are recorded in every county where the bankrupt owns real estate not exempt from execution, and pay the fee for such filing, and he shall receive a compensation of fifty cents for each copy so filed, which, together with the filing fee, shall be paid out of the estate of the bankrupt as a part of the cost and disbursements of the proceedings.

Compensation of Trustees, Receivers and Marshals:

Sec. 48.—a. Trustees shall receive for their services, payable after they are rendered, a fee of five dollars deposited with the clerk at the time the petition is filed in each case, except when a fee is not required from a voluntary bankrupt, and such commissions on all moneys disbursed or turned over to any person including lien holders, by them, as may be allowed by the courts, not to exceed six per centum on the first five hundred dollars or less, four per centum on moneys in excess of five hundred dollars and less than fifteen hundred dollars, two per centum on moneys in excess of fifteen hundred dollars, and less than ten thousand dollars, and one per centum on moneys in excess of ten thousand dollars. And in case of the confirmation of a composition after the trustee has qualified the court may allow him, as compensation, not to exceed one-half of one per centum of the amount to be paid the creditors of such composition.

b. In the event of an estate being administered by three trustees instead of one trustee or by successive trustees, the court shall apportion the fees and commissions between them according to the services actually rendered, so that there shall not be paid to trustees for the administering of any estate a greater amount than one trustee would be entitled to.

c. The court may, in its discretion, withhold all compensation from any trustee who has been removed for cause.

d. Receivers or marshals appointed pursuant to section two, subdivision three, of this act shall receive for their services, payable after they are rendered, compensation by way of commission upon the moneys disbursed or turned over to any person, including lien holders, by them, and also upon the moneys turned over by them or afterwards realized by the trustees from property turned over in kind by them to the trustees, as the court may allow, not to exceed six per centum on the first five hundred dollars or less, four per centum on moneys in excess of five hundred dollars and less than one thousand five hundred dollars, two per centum on moneys in excess of one thousand five hundred dollars and less than ten thousand dollars, and one per centum on moneys in excess of ten thousand dollars: Provided, That in case of the confirmation of a composition such commissions shall not exceed one-half of one per centum of the amount to be paid creditors on such compositions: Provided further, That when the receiver or marshal acts as a mere custodian and does not carry on the business of the bankrupt as provided in clause five of section two of this act, he shall not receive nor be allowed in any form or guise more than two per centum on the first thousand dollars or less, and one-half of one per centum on all above one thousand dollars on moneys subsequently realized from property turned over by him in kind to the trustee; Provided further, That before the allowance of compensation notice of application therefor, specifying the amount asked, shall be given to creditors in the manner indicated in section fifty-eight of this act.

e. Where the business is conducted by trustees, marshals, or receivers, as provided in clause five of section two of this act, the court may allow such officers additional compensation for such services by way of commissions upon the moneys disbursed or turned over to any person, including lien holders, by them, and, in cases of receivers or marshals, also upon the moneys turned over by them or afterwards realized by the trustees from property turned over in kind by them to the trustees; such commissions not to exceed six per centum on the first five hundred dollars or less, four per centum on moneys in excess of five hundred dollars and less than one thousand five hundred dollars, two per centum on moneys in excess of one thousand five hundred dollars and less than ten thousand dollars, and one per centum on moneys in excess of ten thousand dollars: Provided, That in case of the confirmation of a composition such commissions shall not exceed one-half of one per centum of the amount to be paid creditors on such composition: Provided further, That before the allowance of compensation notice of application therefor, specifying the amount asked, shall be given to creditors in the manner indicated in section fifty-eight of this act.

Accounts and Papers of Trustees:
Sec. 49.—a. The accounts and papers of trustees shall be open to the inspection of officers and all parties in interest.

Bonds of Referees and Trustees:
Sec. 50.—a. Referees, before assuming the duties of their offices, and within such time as the district courts of the United States having jurisdiction shall prescribe, shall respectively qualify by entering into bond to the United States in such sum as shall be fixed

by such courts, not to exceed five thousand dollars, with such sureties as shall be approved by such courts, conditioned for the faithful performance of their official duties.

b. Trustees, before entering upon the performance of their official duties, and within ten days after their appointment, or within such further time, not to exceed five days, as the court may permit, shall respectively qualify by entering into bond to the United States, with such sureties as shall be approved by the courts, conditioned for the faithful performance of their official duties.

c. The creditors of a bankrupt estate, at their first meeting after the adjudication, or after a vacancy has occurred in the office of trustee, or after an estate has been reopened, or after a composition has been set aside or a discharge revoked, if there is a vacancy in the office of trustee, shall fix the amount of the bond of the trustee; they may at any time increase the amount of the bond. If the creditors do not fix the amount of the bond of the trustee as herein provided the court shall do so.

d. The court shall require evidence as to the actual value of the property of sureties.

e. There shall be at least two sureties upon each bond.

f. The actual value of the property of the sureties, over and above their liabilities and exemptions, on each bond shall equal at least the amount of such bond.

g. Corporations organized for the purpose of becoming sureties upon bonds, or authorized by law to do so, may be accepted as sureties upon the bonds of referees and trustees whenever the courts are satisfied that the rights of all parties in interest will be thereby amply protected.

h. Bonds of referees, trustees, and designated depositories shall be filed of record in the office of the clerk of the court and may be sued upon in the name of the United States for the use of any person injured by a breach of their conditions.

i. Trustees shall not be liable personally or on their bonds, to the United States, for any penalities or forfeitures incurred by the bankrupts under this Act, of whose estates they are respectively trustees.

j. Joint trustees may give joint or several bonds.

k. If any referee or trustee shall fail to give bond, as herein provided and within the time limited, he shall be deemed to have declined his appointment, and such failure shall create a vacancy in his office.

l. Suits upon referees' bonds shall not be brought subsequent to two years after the alleged breach of the bond.

m. Suits upon trustees' bonds shall not be brought subsequent to two years after the estate has been closed.

Duties of Clerks:

Sec. 51.—a. Clerks shall respectively (1) account for, as for other fees received by them, the clerk's fee paid in each case and such other fees as may be received for certified copies of records which may be prepared for persons other than officers; (2) collect the fees of the clerk, referee, and trustee in each case instituted before filing the petition, except the petition of a proposed voluntary bankrupt which is accompanied by an affidavit stating that the petitioner is without, and can not obtain, the money with which to pay such fees; (3) deliver to the referees upon application all papers which may be referred to them, or, if the offices of such referees are not in the same cities or towns as the offices of such clerks, transmit such papers by mail, and in like manner return papers which were received from such referees after they have been used; (4) and within ten days after each case has been closed pay to the referee, if the case was referred, the fee collected for him, and to the trustee the fee collected for him at the time of filing the petition.

Compensation of Clerks and Marshals:

Sec. 52.—a. Clerks shall respectively receive as full compensation for their services to each estate, a filing fee of ten dollars, except when a fee is not required from a voluntary bankrupt.

b. Marshals shall respectively receive from the estate where an adjudication in bankruptcy is made, except as herein otherwise provided, for the performance of their services in proceedings in bankruptcy, the same fees, and account for them in the same way, as they are entitled to receive for the performance of the same or similar services in other cases in accordance with laws now in force, or such as may be hereafter enacted fixing the compensation of marshals.

Duties of Attorney-General:

Sec. 53.—a. The Attorney-General shall annually lay before Congress statistical tables showing for the whole country, and by States, the number of cases during the year of voluntary and involuntary bankruptcy; the amount of the property of the estates; the dividends paid and the expenses of administering such estates; and such other like information as he may deem important.

Statistics of Bankruptcy Proceedings:

Sec. 54.—a. Officers shall furnish in writing and transmit by mail such information as is within their knowledge, and as may be shown by the records and papers in their possession, to the Attorney-General, for statistical purposes, within ten days after being requested by him to do so.

CHAPTER VI

CREDITORS

Meetings of Creditors:

Sec. 55.—a. The court shall cause the first meeting of the creditors of a bankrupt to be held, not less than ten nor more than thirty days after the adjudication, at the county seat of the county in which the bankrupt has had his principal place of business, resided, or had his domicile; or if that place would be manifestly inconvenient as a place of meeting for the parties in interest, or if the bankrupt is one who does not do business, reside, or have his domicile within the United States, the court shall fix a place for the meeting which is the most convenient for parties in interest. If such meeting should by any mischance not be held within such time, the court shall fix the date, as soon as may be thereafter, when it shall be held.

b. At the first meeting of creditors the judge or referee shall preside and, before proceeding with the other business, may allow or disallow the claims of creditors there presented, and may publicly examine the bankrupt or cause him to be examined at the instance of any creditor.

c. The creditors shall at each meeting take such

steps as may be pertinent and necessary for the promotion of the best interest of the estate and the enforcement of this Act.

d. A meeting of creditors, subsequent to the first one, may be held at any time and place when all of the creditors who have secured the allowance of their claims sign a written consent to hold a meeting at such time and place.

e. The court shall call a meeting of creditors whenever one-fourth or more in number of those who have proven their claims shall file a written request to that effect; if such request is signed by a majority of claims, and contains a request for such meeting to be held at a designated place, the court shall call such meeting at such place within thirty days after the date of the filing of the request.

f. Whenever the affairs of the estate are ready to be closed a final meeting of creditors shall be ordered.

Voters at Meetings of Creditors:
Sec. 56.—a. Creditors shall pass upon matters submitted to them at their meetings by a majority vote in number and amount of claims of all creditors whose claims have been allowed and are present, except as herein otherwise provided.

b. Creditors holding claims which are secured or have priority shall not, in respect to such claims, be entitled to vote at creditors' meetings, nor shall such claims be counted in computing either the number of creditors or the amount of their claims, unless the amounts of such claims exceed the value of such securities or priorities, and then only for such excess.

Proof and Allowance of Claims:

Sec. 57.—a. Proof of claims shall consist of a statement under oath, in writing, signed by a creditor setting forth the claim, the consideration therefor, and whether any, and, if so, what, securities are held therefor, and whether any, and, if so what, payments have been made thereon, and that the sum claimed is justly owing from the bankrupt to the creditor.

b. Whenever a claim is founded upon an instrument of writing, such instrument, unless lost or destroyed, shall be filed with the proof of claim. If such instrument is lost or destroyed, a statement of such fact and of the circumstances of such loss or destruction shall be filed under oath with the claim. After the claim is allowed or disallowed, such instrument may be withdrawn by permission of the court, upon leaving a copy thereof on file with the claim.

c. Claims after being proved may, for the purpose of allowance, be filed by the claimants in the court where the proceedings are pending or before the referee if the case has been referred.

d. Claims which have been duly proved shall be allowed, upon receipt by or upon presentation to the court, unless objection to their allowance shall be made by parties in interest, or their consideration be continued for cause by the court upon its own motion.

e. Claims of secured creditors and those who have priority may be allowed to enable such creditors to participate in the proceedings at creditors' meetings held prior to the determination of the value of their securities or priorities, but shall be allowed for such sums only as to the courts seem to be owing over and above the value of their securities or priorities.

f. Objections to claims shall be heard and determined as soon as the convenience of the court and the best interests of the estates and the claimants will permit.

g. The claims of creditors who have received preferences, voidable under section sixty, subdivision b, or to whom conveyances, transfers, assignments, or encumbrances, void or voidable under section sixty-seven, subdivision e, have been made or given, shall not be allowed unless such creditors shall surrender such preferences, conveyances, transfers, assignments, or encumbrances.

h. The value of securities held by secured creditors shall be determined by converting the same into money according to the terms of the agreement pursuant to which such securities were delivered to such creditors or by such creditors and the trustee, by agreement, arbitration, compromise, or litigation, as the court may direct and the amount of such value shall be credited upon such claims, and a dividend shall be paid only on the unpaid balance.

i. Whenever a creditor, whose claim against a bankrupt estate is secured by the individual undertaking of any person, fails to prove such claim, such person may do so in the creditor's name, and if he discharge such undertaking in whole or in part he shall be subrogated to that extent to the rights of the creditor.

j. Debts owing to the United States, a state, a county, a district, or a municipality as a penalty or forfeiture shall not be allowed, except for the amount of the pecuniary loss sustained by the act, transaction, or proceeding out of which the penalty or forfeiture arose, with reasonable and actual costs occasioned thereby and such interest as may have accrued thereon according to law.

k. Claims which have been allowed may be reconsidered for cause and reallowed or rejected in whole or in part, according to the equities of the case, before but not after the estate has been closed.

l. Whenever a claim shall have been reconsidered and rejected, in whole or in part, upon which a dividend has been paid, the trustee may recover from the creditor the amount of the dividend received upon the claim if rejected in whole, or the proportional part thereof if rejected only in part.

m. The claim of any estate which is being administered in bankruptcy against any like estate may be proved by the trustee and allowed by the court in the same manner and upon like terms as the claims of other creditors.

n. Claims shall not be proved against a bankrupt estate subsequent to one year after the adjudication; or if they are liquidated by litigation and the final judgment therein is rendered within thirty days before or after the expiration of such time, then within sixty days after the rendition of such judgment: Provided, That the right of infants and insane persons without guardians, without notice of the proceedings, may continue six months longer.

Notice to Creditors:

Sec. 58.—a. Creditors shall have at least ten days' notice by mail, to their respective addresses as they appear in the list of creditors of the bankrupt, or as afterwards filed with the papers in the case of the creditors, unless they waive notice in writing of (1) all examinations of the bankrupt; (2) all hearings upon applications for the confirmation of compositions; (3) all meetings of creditors; (4) all proposed sales of property; (5) the declaration and time of payment of dividends; (6) the filing of the final accounts of the trustees and the time when and the place where they will be examined and passed upon; (7) the proposed compromise of any controversy, and (8) the proposed dismissal of the proceedings, and (9) there shall be thirty days' notice of all applications for the discharge of bankrupts.

b. Notice to creditors of the first meeting shall be published at least once and may be published such number of additional times as the court may direct; the last publication shall be at least one week prior to the date fixed for the meeting. Other notices may be published as the court shall direct.

c. All notices shall be given by the referee unless otherwise ordered by the judge.

Who May File and Dismiss Petitions:

Sec. 59.—a. Any qualified person may file a petition to be adjudged a voluntary bankrupt.

b. Three or more creditors who have provable claims against any person which amount in the aggregate, in excess of the value of securities held by them, if any, to five hundred dollars or over; or if all of the creditors of such person are less than twelve in number, the one of such creditors whose claim equals such amount may file a petition to have him adjudged a bankrupt.

c. Petitions shall be filed in duplicate, one copy for the clerk and one for service on the bankrupt.

d. If it be averred in the petition that the creditors of the bankrupt are less than twelve in number, and less than three creditors have joined as petitioners therein, and the answer avers the existence of a large number of creditors, there shall be filed with the answers a list under oath of all the creditors, with their addresses, and thereupon the court shall cause all such creditors to be notified of the pendency of such petition and shall delay the hearing upon such petition for a reasonable time, to the end that parties in interest shall have an opportunity to be heard; if upon such hearing it shall appear that a sufficient number have joined in such petition, or if prior to or during such hearing a sufficient number shall join therein, the case may be proceeded with, but otherwise it shall be dismissed.

e. In computing the number of creditors of a bankrupt for the purpose of determining how many creditors must join in the petition, such creditors as were employed by him at the time of the filing of the petition or are related to him by consanguinity, or affinity within the third degree, as determined by the common law, and have not joined in the petition, shall not be counted.

f. Creditors other than original petitioners may at any time enter their appearance and join in the petition, or file an answer and be heard in opposition to the prayer of the petition.

g. A voluntary or involuntary petition shall not be dismissed by the petitioner or petitioners or for want of prosecution or by consent of parties until after notice to the creditors, and to that end the court shall, before entertaining an application for dismissal, require the bankrupt to file a list, under oath, of all his creditors, with their addresses, and shall cause notice to be sent to all such creditors of the pendency of such application and shall delay the hearing thereon for a reasonable time to allow all creditors and parties in interest opportunity to be heard.

Preferred Creditors:

Sec. 60.—a. A person shall be deemed to have given a preference if, being insolvent, he has, within four months before the filing of the petition, or after the filing of the petition and before the adjudication, procured or suffered a judgment to be entered against himself in favor of any person, or made a transfer of any of his property, and the effect of the enforcement of such judgment or transfer will be to enable any one of his creditors to obtain a greater percentage of his debt than any other of such creditors of the same class. Where the preference consists in a transfer, such period of four months shall not expire until four months after the date of the recording or registering of the transfer, if by law such recording or registering is required.

b. If a bankrupt shall have procured or suffered a judgment to be entered against him in favor of any person or have made a transfer to any of his property, and if, at the time of the transfer, or of the entry of the judgment, or of the recording or registering of the transfer if by law recording or registering thereof is required and being within four months before the filing of the petition in bankruptcy or after the filing thereof and before the adjudication the bankrupt be insolvent and the judgment or transfer then operate as a preference, and the person receiving it or to be benefited thereby, or his agent acting therein shall then have reasonable cause to believe that the enforcement of such judgment or transfer would effect a preference, it shall be voidable by the trustee and he may recover the property or its value from such person. And for the purpose of such recovery, any court of bankruptcy, as hereinbefore defined, and any State court which would have had jurisdiction if bankruptcy had not intervened, shall have concurrent jurisdiction.

c. If a creditor has been preferred, and afterwards in good faith gives the debtor further credit without security of any kind for property which becomes a part of the debtor's estates, the amount of such new credit remaining unpaid at the time of the adjudication in bankruptcy may be set off against the amount which would otherwise be recoverable from him.

d. If a debtor shall, directly or indirectly, in contemplation of the filing of a petition by or against him, pay money or transfer property to an attorney and counselor at law, solicitor in equity, or proctor in admiralty for services to be rendered, the transaction shall be reexamined by the court on petition of the trustee or any creditor and shall only be held valid to the extent of a reasonable amount to be determined by the court, and the excess may be recovered by the trustee for the benefit of the estate.

CHAPTER VII

ESTATES

Depositories for Money:

Sec. 61.—a. Courts of bankruptcy shall designate, by order, banking institutions as depositories for the money of bankrupt estates, as convenient as may be to the residences of trustees, and shall require bonds to the United States, subject to their approval, to be given by such banking institutions, and may from time to time as occasion may require, by like order increase the number of depositories or the amount of any bond or change such depositories.

Expenses of Administering Estates:

Sec. 62.—a. The actual and necessary expenses incurred by officers in the administration of estates shall, except where other provisions are made for their payment, be reported in detail, under oath, and examined and approved or disapproved by the court. If approved, they shall be paid or allowed out of the estates in which they were incurred.

Debts which May be Proved:

Sec. 63.—a. Debts of the bankrupt may be proved and allowed against his estate which are (1) a fixed liability, as evidenced by a judgment or an instrument in writing, absolutely owing at the time of the filing of the petition against him, whether then payable or not, with any interest thereon which would have been recoverable at that date or with a rebate of interest upon such as were not then payable and did not bear interest; (2) due as costs taxable against an involuntary bankrupt who was at the time of the filing of the petition against him plaintiff in a cause of action which would pass to the trustee and which the trustee declines to prosecute after notice; (3) founded upon a claim for taxable costs incurred in good faith by a creditor before the filing of the petition in an action to recover a provable debt; (4) founded upon an open account, or upon a contract express or implied; and (5) founded upon provable debts reduced to judgments after the filing of the petition and before the consideration of the bankrupt's application for a discharge, less costs incurred and interests accrued after the filing of the petition and up to the time of the entry of such judgments.

b. Unliquidated claims against the bankrupt may, pursuant to application to the court, be liquidated in such manner as it shall direct, and may thereafter be proved and allowed against his estate.

Debts Which have Priority:

Sec. 64.—a. The court shall order the trustee to pay all taxes legally due and owing by the bankrupt to the

United States, State, county, district, or municipality in advance of the payment of dividends to creditors, and upon filing the receipts of the proper public officers for such payment he shall be credited with the amount thereof, and in case any question arises as to the amount or legality of any such tax the same shall be heard and determined by the court.

b. The debts to have priority, except as herein provided, and to be paid in full out of bankrupt estates, and the order of payment shall be (1) the actual and necessary cost of preserving the estate subsequent to filing the petition; (2) the filing fees paid by creditors in involuntary cases, and, where property of the bankrupt, transferred or concealed by him either before or after the filing of the petition, shall have been recovered for the benefit of the estate of the bankrupt by the efforts and at the expense of one or more creditors, the reasonable expenses of such recovery; (3) the cost of administration, including the fees and mileage payable to witnesses as now or hereafter provided by the laws of the United States, and one reasonable attorney's fee, for the professional services actually rendered, irrespective of the number of attorneys employed, to the petitioning creditors in involuntary cases, to the bankrupt in involuntary cases while performing the duties herein prescribed, and to the bankrupt in voluntary cases, as the court may allow; (4) wages due to workmen, clerks, traveling or city salesmen, or servants which have been earned within three months before the date of the commencement of proceedings, not to exceed three hundred dollars to each claimant; and (5) debts owing to any person who by the laws of the States or the United States is entitled to priority.

c. In the event of the confirmation being set aside, or a discharge revoked, the property acquired by the bankrupt in addition to his estate at the time the composition was confirmed or the adjudication was made shall be applied to the payment in full of the claims of creditors for property sold to him on credit, in good faith, while such composition or discharge was in force, and the residue, if any, shall be applied to the payment of the debts which were owing at the time of the adjudication.

Declaration and Payment of Dividends:

Sec. 65.—a. Dividends of an equal per centum shall be declared and paid on all allowed claims, except such as have priority or are secured.

b. The first dividend shall be declared within thirty days after the adjudication, if the money of the estate in excess of the amount necessary to pay the debts which have priority and such claims as have not been, but probably will be, allowed equals five per centum or more of such allowed claims. Dividends subsequent to the first shall be declared upon like terms as the first and as often as the amount shall equal ten per centum or more and upon closing the estate. Dividends may be declared oftener and in smaller proportions if the judge shall so order; Provided, That the first dividend shall not include more than fifty per centum of the money of the estate in excess of the amount necessary to pay the debts which have priority and such claims as probably will be allowed; And provided further, That the final dividend shall not be declared within three months after the first dividend shall be declared.

c. The rights of creditors who have received dividends, or in whose favor final dividends have been declared, shall not be affected by the proof and allowance of claims subsequent to the date of such payment or declarations of dividends; but the creditors proving and securing the allowance of such claims shall be paid dividends equal in amount to those already received by the other creditors if the estate equals so much before such other creditors are paid any further dividends.

d. Whenever a person shall have been adjudged a bankrupt by a court without the United States and also by a court of bankruptcy, creditors residing within the United States shall first be paid a dividend equal to that received in the court without the United States by other creditors before creditors who have received a dividend in such courts shall be paid any amounts.

e. A claimant shall not be entitled to collect from a bankrupt estate any greater amount than shall accrue pursuant to the provisions of this Act.

Unclaimed Dividends:

Sec. 66.—a. Dividends which remain unclaimed for six months after the final dividend has been declared shall be paid by the trustee into court.

b. Dividends remaining unclaimed for one year shall, under the direction of the court, be distributed to the creditors whose claims have been allowed but not paid in full, and after such claims have been paid in full the balance shall be paid to the bankrupt: Provided, That in case unclaimed dividends belong to minors such minors may have one year after arriving at majority to claim such dividends.

Liens:

Sec. 67.—a. Claims which for want of record or for other reasons would not have been valid liens as against the claims of the creditors of the bankrupt shall not be liens against his estate.

b. Whenever a creditor is prevented from enforcing his rights as against a lien created, or attempted to be created, by his debtor, who afterwards becomes a bankrupt, the trustee of the estate of such bankrupt shall be subrogated to and may enforce such rights of such creditor for the benefit of the estate.

c. A lien created by or obtained in or pursuant to any suit or proceeding at law or in equity, including an attachment upon mesne process or a judgment by confession, which was begun against a person within four months before the filing of a petition in bankruptcy by or against such person shall be dissolved by the adjudication of such person to be a bankrupt if (1) it appears that said lien was obtained and permitted while the defendant was insolvent and that its existence and enforcement will work a preference, or (2) the party or parties to be benefited thereby had reasonable cause to believe the defendant was insolvent and in contemplation of bankruptcy, or (3) that such lien was sought and permitted in fraud of the provisions of this Act; or if the dissolution of such lien would militate against the best interests of the estate of such person the same shall not be dissolved, but the trustee of the estate of such person, for the benefit of the estate, shall be subrogated to the rights of the holder of such lien and empowered to perfect and enforce the same in his name as trustee with like force and effect as such holder might have done had not bankruptcy proceedings intervened.

d. Liens given or accepted in good faith and not in contemplation of or in fraud upon this Act and for a present consideration which have been recorded according to law, if record thereof was necessary in order to impart notice, shall, to the extent of such present consideration only, not be affected by this Act.

e. That all conveyances, transfers, assignments, or encumbrances of his property, or any part thereof, made or given by a person adjudged a bankrupt under the provisions of this Act subsequent to the passage of this Act and within four months prior to the filing of the petition, with the intent and purpose on his part to hinder, delay, or defraud his creditors, or any of them, shall be null and void as against the creditors of such debtor, except as to purchasers in good faith and for a present fair consideration; and all property of the debtor conveyed, transferred, assigned, or encumbered as aforesaid shall, if he be adjudged a bankrupt, and the same is not exempt from execution and liability for debts by the law of his domicile, be and remain a part of the assets and estate of the bankrupt and shall pass to his said trustee, whose duty it shall be to recover and reclaim the same by legal proceedings or otherwise for the benefit of the creditors. And all conveyances, transfers, or encumbrances of his property made by a debtor at any time within four months prior to the filing of the petition against him, and while insolvent, which are held null and void as against the creditors of such debtor by the laws of the State, Territory, or District in which such property is situate, shall be deemed null and void under this Act against the creditors of such debtor if he be adjudged a bankrupt, and such property shall pass to the assignee and be by him reclaimed and recovered for the benefit of the creditors of the bankrupt. For the purpose of such recovery any court of bankruptcy as hereinbefore defined, and any State court which would have had jurisdiction if bankruptcy had not intervened, shall have concurrent jurisdiction.

f. That all levies, judgments, attachments, or other liens, obtained through legal proceedings against a person who is insolvent, at any time within four months prior to the filing of a petition in bankruptcy against him, shall be deemed null and void in case he is adjudged a bankrupt, and the property affected by the levy, judgment, attachment, or other lien shall be deemed wholly discharged and released from the same, and shall pass to the trustee as a part of the estate of the bankrupt, unless the court shall, on due notice, order that the right under such levy, judgment, attachment, or other lien shall be preserved for the benefit of the estate; and thereupon the same may pass to and shall be preserved by the trustee for the benefit of the estate as aforesaid. And the court may order such conveyance as shall be necessary to carry the purposes of this section into effect: Provided, That nothing herein contained shall have the effect to destroy or impair the title obtained by such levy, judgment, attachment or other lien, of a bona fide purchaser for value who shall have acquired the same without notice or reasonable cause for inquiry.

Set-Offs and Counterclaims:

Sec. 68.—a. In all cases of mutual debts or mutual credits between the estates of a bankrupt and a creditor the account shall be stated and one debt shall be set off against the other, and the balance only shall be allowed or paid.

b. A set-off or counterclaim shall not be allowed in favor of any debtor of the bankrupt which (1) is not provable against the estate; or (2) was purchased by or transferred to him after the filing of the petition, or within four months before such filing, with a view to such use and with knowledge or notice that such bankrupt was insolvent, or had committed an act of bankruptcy.

Possession of Property:

Sec. 69.—a. A judge may, upon satisfactory proof, by affidavit, that a bankrupt against whom an involuntary petition has been filed and is pending has committed an act of bankruptcy, or has neglected or is neglecting, or is about to so neglect his property that it has thereby deteriorated or is thereby deteriorating or is about thereby to deteriorate in value, issue a warrant to the marshal to seize and hold it subject to further orders. Before such warrant is issued the petitioners applying therefor shall enter into a bond in such an amount as the judge shall fix, with such sureties as he shall approve, conditioned to indemnify such bankrupt for such damages as he shall sustain in the event such seizure shall prove to have been wrongfully obtained. Such property shall be released, if such bankrupt shall give bond in a sum which shall be fixed by the judge, with such sureties as he shall approve, conditioned to turn over such property, or pay the value thereof in money to the trustee, in the event he is adjudged a bankrupt pursuant to such petition.

Title to Property:

Sec. 70.—a. The trustee of the estate of a bankrupt, upon his appointment and qualification, and his successor or successors, if he shall have one or more, upon his or their appointment and qualification, shall in turn be vested by operation of law with the title of the bankrupt, as of the date he was adjudged a bankrupt, except in so far as it is to property which is exempt, to all (1) documents relating to his property; (2) interests in patents, patent rights, copyrights, and trade-marks; (3) powers which he might have exercised for his own benefit, but not those which he might have exercised for some other person; (4) property transferred by him in fraud of his creditors; (5) property which prior to the filing of the petition he could by any means have transferred or which might have been levied upon and sold under judicial process against him: Provided, That when any bankrupt shall have any insurance policy which has a cash surrender value payable to himself, his estate or personal representatives, he may, within thirty days after the cash surrender value has been ascertained and stated to the trustee by the company issuing the same, pay or secure to the trustee the sum so ascertained and stated, and continue to hold, own, and carry such policy free from the claims of the creditors participating in the distribution of his estate under the bankruptcy proceedings, otherwise the policy shall pass to the trustee as assets; and (6) rights of action arising upon contracts or from the unlawful taking or detention of or injury to, his property.

b. All real and personal property belonging to bankrupt estates shall be appraised by three disinterested appraisers; they shall be appointed by, and report to, the court. Real and personal property shall, when practicable, be sold subject to the approval of the court; it shall not be sold otherwise than subject to the approval of the court for less than seventy-five per centum of its appraised value.

c. The title to property of a bankrupt estate which has been sold, as herein provided, shall be conveyed to the purchaser by the trustee.

d. Whenever a composition shall be set aside, or discharge revoked, the trustee shall, upon his appointment and qualification, be vested as herein provided with the title to all of the property of the bankrupt as of the date of the final decree setting aside the composition or revoking the discharge.

e. The trustee may avoid any transfer by the bankrupt of his property which any creditor of such bankrupt might have avoided, and may recover the property so transferred, or its value, from the person to whom it was transferred, unless he was a bona fide holder for value prior to the date of the adjudication. Such property may be recovered or its value collected from whoever may have received it, except a bona fide holder for value. For the purpose of such recovery any court of bankruptcy, as hereinbefore defined, and any State court which would have had jurisdiction if bankruptcy had not intervened, shall have concurrent jurisdiction.

f. Upon the confirmation of a composition offered by a bankrupt, the title to his property shall thereupon revest in him.

Sec. 71. That the clerks of the several districts of the United States shall prepare and keep in their respective offices complete and convenient indexes of all petitions and discharges in bankruptcy heretofore or hereafter filed in the said courts, and shall, when requested so to do, issue certificates of search certifying as to whether or not any such petitions or discharges have been filed; and said clerks shall be entitled to receive for such certificates the same fees as now allowed by law for certificates as to judgments in said courts: Provided, That said bankruptcy indexes and dockets shall at all times be open to inspection and examination by all persons or corporations without any fee or charge therefor.

Sec. 72. That neither the referee, receiver, marshal, nor trustee shall in any form or guise receive, nor shall the court allow them, any other or further compensation for his services than expressly authorized and prescribed in this act.

The Time When This Act Shall go into Effect:
a. This Act shall go into full force and effect upon its passage: Provided, however, That no petition for voluntary bankruptcy shall be filed within one month of the passage thereof, and no petition for involuntary bankruptcy shall be filed within four months of the passage thereof.

b. Proceedings commenced under state insolvency laws before the passage of this Act shall not be affected by it.

Sec. 14 of the amendatory act of 1910 provides as follows: "That the provisions of this amendatory act shall not apply to bankruptcy cases pending when this act takes effect, but such cases shall be adjudicated and disposed of conformably to the provisions of said act approved July first, eighteen hundred and ninety-eight, as amended by said act approved February fifth, nineteen hundred and three and as further amended by said act approved June fifteenth, nineteen hundred and six."

APPENDIX

REQUIREMENTS OF EACH STATE AS TO CONDITIONAL SALES CONTRACTS

Alabama:

Contracts must be in writing, signed by the buyer, but need not be signed by the seller. No witnesses, acknowledgment or proof are required, but must be recorded as against third persons, unless the amount involved is less than $200.00 and the county where the record is to be made has more than 80,000 inhabitants (for instance, Jefferson, Mobile and Montgomery Counties), where the contracts need not be recorded or filed. It is necessary to record all contracts covering railroad equipment.

Arizona:

Contracts must be in writing, signed by both parties, but witnesses are unnecessary. Contracts must be filed to be good as against third parties, and if the original is filed no acknowledgment is necessary, but if the copy is filed, the original must be acknowledged by the buyer. All sales of railroad equipment under conditional sales must be signed, recorded and acknowledged.

Arkansas:

Contracts must be in writing, signed by the buyer, but it is not necessary that they be signed by the seller. No acknowledgment or witnesses are required, and it need not be filed or recorded unless the property becomes irremovably attached to real estate. All contracts covering railroad equipment must be signed and acknowledged by the buyer and recorded.

California:

Contracts must be in writing and signed by the buyer, but need not be signed by the seller. No witnesses, acknowledgment or proof are required. Neither is it necessary to file or record the contract to hold title as against third persons.

Colorado:

It is the practice in this state to use chattel mortgages entirely as the only safe method of preserving security to the seller as against the rights of third parties. The chattel mortgage used in Colorado in proper form, duly signed, acknowledged and recorded, eliminates all questions. Railroad equipment may be sold on a conditional sales contract, if in writing, acknowledged by the buyer and recorded or filed and is good as against third persons.

Connecticut:

Contracts must be in writing and signed by the buyer, but it is not necessary for the seller to sign. Witnesses are not required, but the contract must be acknowledged and recorded to preserve rights as against third persons. Railroad equipment may be sold on a conditional sales contract if signed and acknowledged by all parties and recorded.

Delaware:

Contracts should be in writing, signed by the buyer, but need not be signed by the seller. Witnesses, acknowledgments or other proof not required, neither is it necessary to record or file to protect the seller against all parties, with the possible exception of a landlord's lien for the rent of the premises where the property sold is located. Sales of railroad equipment may be on a contract if acknowledged and must be recorded.

District of Columbia:

Contracts must be in writing, signed by the buyer, but not necessary to be signed by the seller. Witnesses are unnecessary. If purchase price is over $100.00 contract must be acknowledged by the buyer and recorded. If the amount is less than $100.00 contract is good as against all persons, unacknowledged and unrecorded, excepting possibly a lien of the landlord for rent where the property is located. There is no special statute on railroad equipment.

Florida:

Contracts should be in writing, signed by the buyer. For two years following date of sale it is not necessary to record to protect the seller against all persons, excepting a landlord's lien for rent of the premises where the property is located. After two years from date of sale has elapsed the seller must sign the contract before two subscribing witnesses, acknowledge it and record it. The two year limit does not apply to sales of railroad equipment, in which case the contract should be signed by all parties and recorded to hold title as against third persons.

Georgia:

Contracts must be in writing, signed by the buyer, but need not be signed by the seller. They must be acknowledged by the buyer or have a single witness to the buyer's signature, who can later prove the contract by oath, so that it may be recorded. All contracts should be witnessed and the salesman may act as the witness, unless he signs the contract on behalf of the seller, in which case an independent, disinterested witness should be procured. Contracts must be recorded. Sales of railroad equipment should be on contract, signed by all parties, with witnesses to the buyer's signature, and should be recorded.

Idaho:

Contracts should be in writing and signed by the seller, but need not be signed by the buyer. No witnesses are necessary, and the contract need not be acknowledged, proven, filed or recorded. Where railroad equipment is sold both parties must sign, the buyer must acknowledge it or it must be proved as deeds are proved, and recorded.

Illinois:

Conditional sales contracts are not good as against third persons in this state under any circumstances, but an order form of contract should be used providing for the giving of a chattel mortgage upon the property to secure the purchase price. Such mortgage must be signed by the buyer and be acknowledged and recorded. Where railroad equipment is sold a conditional sales contract may be used, which must be acknowledged by the buyer and be recorded or filed, and is then good as against third persons.

Indiana:

Contracts must be in writing, signed by the buyer but need not be signed by the seller. Witnesses are not necessary; neither is it necessary to acknowledge, prove, record or file. Sales of railroad equipment can be made on conditional sales contract if signed and acknowledged by the buyer and recorded.

Iowa:

Contracts must be in writing and signed by both parties; witnesses are not necessary, but the contract must be recorded, and either party may acknowledge for that purpose. Railroad equipment can be sold on contract if acknowledged by the buyer and recorded.

Kansas:

Contracts must be in writing, signed by the buyer, but need not be signed by the seller. Witnesses are not necessary. The original or true copy must be filed to be valid as against third persons. It is not necessary to prove or acknowledge the same. Railroad equipment can be sold on such contract if executed by all parties, acknowledged by the buyer and proven as deeds are proven, and recorded.

Kentucky:

Contracts must be in writing, signed by the buyer and must be acknowledged by the buyer or be proven by the oath of either of two witnesses who signed the contract at the time of purchase, and must be recorded. Salesman may act as one witness if he does not sign on behalf of the seller. Sales of railroad equipment must be acknowledged by the buyer or be proven by a witness, and be recorded.

Louisiana:

Conditional sales contracts as against third persons are not recognized in this state. A lease, with the option to purchase, should be used, which need not be acknowledged, proven or recorded, and which protects against all claims except landlord's lien for rent of the premises where the property is located. Railroad equipment, however, may be sold on a conditional sales contract, signed by all parties, acknowledged by the buyer, or proven as deeds are required to be proven, and be recorded. Such contracts are good as against third persons.

Maine:

Contracts must be in writing, signed by the buyer, but need not be signed by the seller. Witnesses are not necessary, neither is acknowledgment or proof required, but contract must be recorded. Railroad equipment sold under conditional sales contracts must be signed by all parties, acknowledged by the buyer or proven as deeds are required to be proven, and must be recorded.

Maryland:

Contracts must be in writing, signed by the buyer, but need not be signed by the seller. Witnesses unnecessary, but contract or memorandum thereof must be recorded to be good as against third persons without notice. No proof or acknowledgment is required, and if the contract is recorded before the property is moved upon a landlord's premises it is good as against his lien for rent. Sales of railroad equipment must be on contracts signed by all parties, acknowledged by the buyer, and recorded in the same manner as a deed to real estate.

Massachusetts:

Contracts must be in writing and signed by all parties thereto. Witness, proof or acknowledgment are not required, but if the property becomes attached to real estate as a fixture then the contract should be recorded to protect the seller against mortgagees, purchasers or grantees of said real estate; otherwise, it is unnecessary to record. Sales of railroad equipment must be on contracts, signed by all parties, acknowledged by the buyer and recorded.

Michigan:

Contracts must be in writing and signed by the buyer but need not be signed by the seller. No acknowledgment, witnesses or proof are required, and it need not be recorded or filed unless the property is delivered to a retailer for the purpose of reselling the same, in which case the contract must be filed to be good as against third persons. Railroad equipment contracts must be acknowledged by the buyer and must be recorded.

Minnesota:

Contracts must be in writing, and must be signed by the buyer, but need not be signed by the seller. No acknowledgment, witnesses or proof are required, but the contract must be filed. Railway equipment contracts must be signed and acknowledged by the buyer and must be recorded.

Mississippi:

Contracts must be in writing and signed by the buyer, but need not be signed by the seller, and are good for three years from date without recording or filing, except as against a landlord's lien for rent of the premises where the property is located, but unless recorded are not good as against creditors of those transacting business as traders or otherwise with the addition of the word, "Agent," "Factor," "& Company," "& Co." or like words and who fail to disclose the principal or partner by a sign easily read, placed conspicuously on the premises where the business is transacted, or who transact business in their own name without any such addition. In order to record the contract there must be one subscribing witness who takes oath that he saw the buyer execute. The salesman may be the witness unless he signs on behalf of the seller. All contracts taken in Mississippi should be witnessed so that later they may be proved and recorded if necessary. Railway equipment contracts must be signed and acknowledged by the buyer and must be recorded.

Missouri:

Contracts must be in writing and signed by the buyer but need not be signed by the seller. It is not necessary to record the contract, nor is it necessary to have it witnessed, but it is better to file a copy to protect the seller. To record a contract it would be necessary to have the buyer acknowledge it in person or have one subscribing witness prove the contract. Sales of railway equipment must be signed by all parties, acknowledged by the buyer and recorded.

Montana:

Contracts must be in writing, signed by the buyer, but need not be signed by the seller. No acknowledgment, witnesses or other proof are required, but the contract should be filed. Contracts for railway equipment must be signed by all parties, acknowledged or proved the same as a deed to real estate, and must be recorded.

Nebraska:

Contracts must be in writing, signed by the buyer, but need not be signed by the seller. No acknowledgment, witnesses or proof are necessary, but the contract must be filed. In order to file contracts in this state the seller must attach to the copy to be filed an affidavit containing his name and the name of the buyer, a description of the property and its value and also the full and true interest of the seller therein. Railway contracts must be signed by all parties, acknowledged by the buyer or proven as deeds to real estate are proven, and recorded.

Nevada:

Contracts must be in writing, signed by the buyer, but need not be signed by the seller. No acknowledgment, witnesses, proof, filing or recording are necessary. Railway equipment contracts must be signed by all parties, acknowledged by the buyer, and recorded.

New Hampshire:

Contracts must be in writing and signed by the buyer, but need not be signed by the seller. No witnesses are necessary. Unless the property is household furniture, the contract must be recorded. No acknowledgment is necessary to record it. All parties, however, must make affidavit, setting forth the nature of the transaction. Railway equipment contracts must be signed by all parties and acknowledged by the buyer, but no affidavit is necessary. Such contracts must be proven as deeds are proven and must be recorded.

New Jersey:

Contracts must be in writing and signed by the buyer, but need not be signed by the seller. It should be acknowledged by the buyer or be witnessed by one who can prove the buyer's signature and then recorded. The salesman can act as witness, unless he signs on behalf of the seller. If the buyer is a corporation the corporate seal should be impressed upon the contract. Railway equipment contracts must be acknowledged by the buyer and be recorded.

New Mexico:

Contracts must be in writing, signed by both the buyer and the seller, but it is not necessary to have it witnessed, though it must be acknowledged by the buyer or the seller and be filed or recorded.

New York:

Contracts must be in writing, signed by the buyer, and need not be acknowledged by either party nor be signed or proven by a subscribing witness, but must be filed. If the property is attached to a building the contract should contain a description of the building by street and number. Railway equipment contracts must be acknowledged by the buyer and be recorded.

North Carolina:

Contracts must be in writing, signed by the buyer, but need not be signed by the seller. One witness to the buyer's signature is necessary. Contract should be acknowledged by the buyer or a subscribing witness, and must be registered. The salesman taking the order may act as a witness, unless he signs on behalf of the buyer. Railway equipment contracts must be in writing and acknowledged by either party and must be recorded.

North Dakota:

Contracts must be in writing and signed by the buyer, but need not be signed by the seller. The original or an authenticated copy must be filed, but it need not be acknowledged or proven in order to be filed. There is some confusion on the point of witnesses, and the only safe rule is to have two witnesses to the buyer's signature. Railway equipment contracts must be in writing, acknowledged and recorded.

Ohio:

Contracts must be in writing, signed by the buyer, but need not be signed by the seller. No acknowledgment, witnesses or proof are required, but a copy of the contract must be filed and to it must be attached an affidavit of the seller, stating the amount of the claim. Railway equipment contracts must be recorded or filed, but no acknowledgment or proof is required.

Oklahoma:

Contracts must be in writing and signed by the buyer, but need not be signed by the seller. A copy of it must be filed but need not be acknowledged or witnessed. Railway equipment contracts must be in writing, executed by all parties, acknowledged by the buyer or proved as deeds are proved, and recorded.

Oregon:

Contracts must be in writing, signed by the buyer, but need not be signed by the seller. No acknowledgment, witnesses or proof are required. Unless the property is attached to real estate as a fixture, the contract need not be filed or recorded. If the property is attached to real estate as a fixture, the contract in full describing the personal property and describing the real estate must be filed within ten days after the property attaches to the real estate in order to be good as against third persons. Railway equipment contracts must be acknowledged by the buyer and be recorded.

Pennsylvania:

Contracts must be in writing but should be in the form of a lease or bailment, with option to purchase, which does not require a subscribing witness and need not be acknowledged, proved, filed or recorded. Such an instrument is good as against all third persons, excepting possibly a landlord's lien for rent upon the premises where the property is located. If the property is attached to real estate a conditional sales contract in writing may be used and must be recorded. Railway equipment contracts must be in writing, acknowledged, and recorded.

Rhode Island:

Contracts must be in writing, signed by the buyer, but need not be signed by the seller. No acknowledgment, witnesses, proof, filing or recording are necessary. Railway equipment contracts must be in writing, executed by all parties, acknowledged by the buyer, proven as deeds are proven, and recorded.

South Carolina:

Contracts must be in writing, signed by the buyer, but need not be signed by the seller, and also must be recorded or filed. Every contract should have two subscribing witnesses. If for less than $100.00 contract may be filed without witnesses proving under oath. If over $100.00, before recording it is necessary that one witness make oath that he saw the buyer sign.

The salesman may act as witness, unless he signs on behalf of the seller. Railway equipment contracts must be in writing, signed by all parties, witnessed properly as to buyer's signature and recorded.

South Dakota:

Contracts must be in writing, signed by the buyer, but need not be signed by the seller. No acknowledgment is required, but contract must be filed. There is some confusion as to witnesses, and the safer plan is to have two witnesses. The salesman may sign as one witness unless he signs on behalf of the seller. Railway equipment contracts must be in writing, acknowledged and recorded.

Tennessee:

Contracts must be in writing, signed by the buyer, but need not be signed by the seller. No witness is necessary. It is also unnecessary to acknowledge, prove, file or record. Railway equipment contracts must be in writing, acknowledged and recorded.

Texas:

Contracts must be in writing and signed by the buyer, but need not be signed by the seller. Contracts must be filed. If the original is filed no witness is required, but if a copy is filed the original must have been witnessed by two persons or have been acknowledged by the buyer. Railway equipment contracts must be in writing and must be recorded, but there is no requirement for acknowledgment or proof.

Utah:

Contracts must be in writing and signed by the buyer, but need not be signed by the seller. No acknowledgment, witnesses or proof are required, and the contract need not be filed or recorded. Railway equipment contracts must be in writing, signed by all parties, acknowledged by the buyer, and recorded.

Vermont:

Contracts must be in writing, signed by the buyer, but need not be signed by the seller. Witnesses not required, neither is it necessary that it be acknowledged or proved, but the original must be recorded. Railway equipment contracts must be executed by all parties, acknowledged by the buyer, proved as deeds to real estate are proved, and recorded.

Virginia:

Contracts must be in writing and signed by all parties. No witnesses or acknowledgment are necessary. A memorandum of the contract must be recorded. This memorandum is taken by the recording officer from the original. Most recording officers in this state will accept a certified or sworn copy, but if the original is demanded it must be sent. Six essential items are necessary for the clerk to make the memorandum: (1) Date, (2) Amount, (3) Date of maturity, (4) Terms, (5) Description, (6) Names of buyer and seller. Railway equipment contracts must be in writing, acknowledged by the buyer as a deed to real estate is acknowledged, and recorded.

Washington:
Contracts must be in writing, signed by all parties. Witnesses are unnecessary, and no acknowledgment or proof is required. The original or a copy must be filed within ten days after the buyer takes possession. Railway equipment contracts must be acknowledged by the buyer as a deed is acknowledged, and recorded.

West Virginia:
Contracts must be in writing and signed by the buyer, but need not be signed by the seller. No acknowledgment, witnesses or proof are necessary. A notice of reservation of title must be recorded and such notice may be signed by the seller. Railway equipment contracts must be in writing, properly signed and acknowledged.

Wisconsin:
Contracts must be in writing, signed by all parties. If the property is household furniture, a copy must be delivered to the buyer at the time of sale and all payments made on such contracts must be endorsed on such copy if the buyer demands it. No witnesses or acknowledgment are required. Copies of all contracts must be filed. Railway equipment contracts must be

in writing and must be recorded, but need not be acknowledged or proved.

Wyoming:

Contracts must be in writing and signed by the buyer, but need not be signed by the seller. No acknowledgment or witnesses are required. A copy of the contract must have attached to it an affidavit of the seller, stating the names of the buyer and the seller, and giving a description of the property, with a statement of the interest of the seller therein, and must be recorded. Railway equipment contracts must be signed by all parties, acknowledged by the buyer, and recorded.

FORMS OF CONDITIONAL SALES CONTRACTS

SHORT FORM, CONDITIONAL SALE CONTRACT

INDIANAPOLIS, Ind., Aug. 14, 1918.

GEM FURNITURE CO.,
City.

Please deliver, at my address shown below, the following:
One No. 518 Rocking Chair,

....
....
for which, delivered, I will pay you the sum of fifteen ($15.00) dollars, as follows:
Five ($5.00) dollars cash with order; five ($5.00) dollars, September 1, 1918, and five ($5.00) dollars November 1, 1918,

....

It is agreed that you shall not relinquish your title to said chair but shall remain the sole owner thereof until the full purchase price above stated is paid to you in money, and that, in case of default, you may, at your option, remove said chair without legal process, all claims for damages and exemptions being hereby waived.

There are no conditions whatever, not stated in this contract.

....
(Signature.)

....
(Address.)

SIMPLE FORM OF CONDITIONAL SALE

....
(Address and Date.)

To ....

....

Please ship, as soon as convenient, as per shipping directions below, the following:

....
....

(Herein describe property)

for which, delivered, f. o. b................., I will pay you the sum of.............................dollars ($..........)....
....
....

(Hereinabove state terms of payment)

It is agreed that you shall not relinquish your title to said......
............................but shall remain the sole owner thereof until the full purchase price above stated is paid to you in money; and if notes are given, until all said notes are actually paid in full. Failure to pay any of said installments or notes when due shall cause any unpaid balance to become due and payable immediately, at your option.

Should you deem yourself unsafe or at any risk, then you may remove said property without legal processes, and all claims for damages on account of such removal are hereby waived; said property not to be removed by us from our place of business or residence until the purchase price is paid in full.

This order is given subject to your approval, and it is expressly understood that there is no agreement relating to said property not herein stated, and the undersigned agrees to accept and pay for said property in accordance with this contract.

....
(*Signature.*)

....
(*City.*)

....
(*State.*)

Shipped to ....
....

PENNSYLVANIA LEASE FORM OF CONTRACT

The Gem Piano Company of Philadelphia, Pennsylvania, hereinafter called the party of the first part, hereby leases unto John Brown, residing at 1020 First St., Philadelphia, Pennsylvania, party of the second part, for the term of................One upright Piano, Style........, No............made by............ on the following terms:

Party of the second part covenants and agrees to pay to the party of the first part at its place of business in said city of Philadelphia, on the date of this lease,......................dollars and on the............day of each and every month thereafter........ ....dollars in lawful money, as rental for said piano.

Upon the termination of this lease, the party of the second part agrees to return said piano to the party of the first part in as good condition as when received, natural wear and tear excepted, and upon the redelivery of said piano hereby leased the party of the second part shall have the option of purchasing the same for the sum of............ dollars.

The party of the second part agrees not to remove said piano out of his present residence nor to sublet the same, and agrees to keep it in good condition and repair as his own expense and to keep it insured against loss and damage by fire in the sum of............ dollars for the benefit of the first party.

It is further agreed between the parties hereto that upon failure of the party of the second part to keep or perform any of the agreements or covenants by him to be kept or performed or upon default of any monthly rental herein provided for that the party of the first part may, without process of law, enter and retake possession of said piano wherever found, and five days after each and every default in the payment of rent herein provided for, and forthwith on every other breach of covenant, the party of the first part may enter a judgment against the second party for all rent due and unpaid and the term of this lease shall then terminate and end, and for entering and confessing said judgment or judgments, with costs of suit and attorneys' fees of $10.00 in each case in any court, without appeal, writ of error or stay of execution, and with a waiver of all exemption laws, this lease or a copy thereof shall be a sufficient warrant of anyone.

IN WITNESS WHEREOF, the said parties have signed and caused their respective seals to be duly affixed hereunto, this...... ......day of................, 1918.

........................(SEAL)
........................(SEAL)

Signed, sealed and delivered
in the presence of
....
Landlord...........
....

Occupation....................
Employer,....................
Business address..............
Lease No.....................

MACHINERY FORM OF CONDITIONAL SALE CONTRACT

.....................1918.

To ....
 (*Name of Purchaser.*)
....
 (*Address.*)
 We hereby propose to furnish and deliver, f. o. b............,
the following...
....
....
(*Herein describe the property*)
shipment to be made to purchaser via..........................
at ....on or about..................
....

The property herein specified is guaranteed by us to be well made, of good material, and in a workmanlike manner; and upon evidence of any defect in workmanship or material within one year from date of shipment thereof this company will replace such defective parts free of charge, f. o. b............, but this company will not be liable for repairs or alterations unless the same are made with our written consent and approval. This company will not be liable for damages nor delays caused by such defective material or workmanship, and it is agreed that its liability under all guarantees is expressly limited to the replacing of parts failing through defects in workmanship or material, free of charge, f. o. b. its factory, within the time and in the manner aforesaid. Parts claimed to be defective are to be returned to us at our option, transporation prepaid.

Additional Equipment. The following equipment is included in the purchase price of this proposal and shall be considered a part thereof:..
....
....
....
We propose to furnish the property as specified herein for the sum

of................dollars ($............) to be paid at the company's office shown herein, as follows:
......................dollars ($.......) cash with order,
......................dollars ($......) upon shipment, sight-draft with bill of lading attached, balance..................
....
....

All deferred payments are to be evidenced by negotiable notes payable to the order of this company, dated and delivered as of the date of shipment and to bear interest from said date at the rate of ....per cent per annum.

THIS PROPOSAL IS MADE UPON THE FOLLOWING CONDITIONS:

That the title and ownership of the property herein specified shall remain in this company until final payment therefor has been made in full as above provided, and in the event that notes are taken at any time, representing deferred payments or any balance that may be due, or in the event that any judgment is taken on account of or on any part of the purchase price, the title to such property shall not pass until such notes so given or extensions thereof or such judgment taken are fully paid in money and satisfied. This company shall have the right to discount or transfer any of said notes, and the title or right of possession in and to said property shall pass thereby to the legal holder of said notes.

You shall take all such legal steps as may be required by the laws of your state for the preservation of this company's title as herein provided, and in the event of any default by you in making any of said payments when due as above provided, the full amount of the purchase price shall, at the election of this company, become immediately due and payable, in which event this company, or its agents or representatives, shall have the right to take possession of said property or any part thereof, wherever found, without process of law, and shall not be held liable for such seizure, and this company may, at its election, upon written notice to you, deposited in the mails ten (10) days prior thereto, addressed to you at your last known address, sell said property or any part thereof, at public or private sale, and at which sale it shall be optional with this company to bid for and purchase this property or any part thereof. This company shall retain so much of the proceeds of said sale necessary to satisfy the balance remaining due, together with costs of such removal and sale, and any excess shall be paid to you. Should the proceeds of said sale not cover the balance remaining due this company, together with the costs of removal and sale, you shall pay the deficiency to this company forthwith after such sale. The said property shall be and remain strictly personal property and retain its character as such, no matter whether on permanent foundation or in what manner affixed or attached to any building or structure or what may be the consequences of its being removed from such foundation, building or structure or for what purpose the property may be used.

That the receipt of the property when delivered to you or to your agents shall constitute a waiver of all claims for damages by reason of any delay, and that you will make good to us any loss or damage to said property caused by fire or otherwise from the time of delivery to you, as herein stated, until the said property is fully paid for, as provided herein.

In the event that it is necessary to employ an attorney in the collection of any moneys due under this contract, you agree to pay attorneys' fees and all other expenses incurred in connection therewith.

As a further consideration, you will pay us twenty (20%) per cent of the purchase price stated in this proposal, as agreed liquidated damages in the event of your refusal to receive said property when delivered or in the event of this proposal's being countermanded by you after having been accepted by you.

It is expressly understood that this proposal made in duplicate, contains all agreements pertaining to the property herein specified, there being no verbal understanding whatsoever, and when signed by the purchaser and approved by an executive officer of this company it becomes a contract binding the parties hereto.

Delivery of all items in this proposal is contingent upon and subject to strikes, accidents, acts or demands of the government in times of war or national emergency, and all other causes beyond our control, and is not guaranteed.

Respectfully submitted,
NATIONAL MACHINERY CO.,
By....................
(*Salesman sign here*)

The above proposal is hereby accepted this............day of ...., 1918.

Signed in the presence of

....

....

....
(*Purchaser sign here*)

Approved,

NATIONAL MACHINERY CO.,

By...................

NOTE.—This contract has been used by machinery dealers with a great deal of success. It covers practically every contingency that might arise. In addition to what is stated in the contract, provision should be made to show the test that the machinery was given before shipment, the specifications of the machinery should be printed in, and care should be taken to carefully designate who is to superintend the installation, and a clause should be inserted that if the company is to superintend erection or installation, if the company's representative is delayed through any fault of the buyer, the buyer is to pay for loss of time.

Particular attention is called to the guarantee, as an unlimited guarantee frequently makes the seller liable for contingent damages. A mere statement that the machinery is guaranteed is not sufficient, as in case a defect should occur,—for instance such as the fly-wheel becoming detached from a moving engine—the contingent damages might be large, but if the liability of the seller is strictly limited to the replacing of defective parts by the terms of the contract itself, no court or jury could impose excessive damages, regardless of the nature of the damages caused by any defect.

The contract, as will be noted, permits the seller to take notes, which agreement does not pass title, except in one or two states where the law provides that the negotiation of such notes passes title.

The title clause is definite, and specifies the procedure in case of default.

Furthermore, frequently machinery is not delivered at the time expected, but the clause that the receipt of the property shall constitute a waiver of all claims for damages by reason of any delay compels the buyer to either accept the machinery when it is offered for delivery or promptly reject it and pursue his remedy for damages. Most buyers will accept the property even though there has been a delay, and this clause relieves the seller from damages in that event.

The contract also provides a penalty in case of cancellation, which is of somewhat doubtful legal value but which nevertheless more securely binds the purchaser, and provision is made for attorneys' fees in the event that attorneys must be employed.

FORM OF CONTRACT USED IN SELLING ENGINES

NATIONAL MACHINERY CO.
(Incorporated)

GENERAL ENGINE PROPOSAL

........................19...

National Machinery Co., a corporation (hereinafter designated as the Company), proposes to furnish and deliver to..............
.............................of............................
(*hereinafter designated as the Purchaser*), subject to the terms and conditions hereinafter set forth, the following machinery and materials:

State Quantity Here	State H. P. Here.	
....	....	
....	....	H. P. Nat. Mach. Co. Type..Style..Engine.
....	....	H. P. Nat. Mach. Co. Type..Style..Engine.
....	....	H. P. Nat. Mach. Co. Type..Style..Engine.

in accordance with the specifications attached hereto and made a part of this proposal, as follows:

Specification No. 1 date......Specification No. 2 date........
Specification No. 3 date......Specification No. 4 date........
Specification No. 5 date......Specification No. 6 date........

DELIVERY. The Company will deliver the said machinery and materials f. o. b. cars its factory, (........) about ....but said date of delivery is not guaranteed by the Company.

HORSE POWER. The engine specified herein shall be tested by the Company at its factory, before shipment and the Company guarantees said engine shall develop............actual horse power at such test.

ERECTION. When preparations are complete, ready for such erection, and at the request of the Purchaser, the Company shall furnish a competent Engineer (at $...... a day and expenses) at the...... ......expense, who shall superintend the erection of the machinery and do all work requiring skilled labor. The Purchaser shall erect the proper and necessary foundations and buildings immediately upon the arrival of such machinery and shall furnish all needed common labor, cartage and materials necessary for such erection and operation, rendering at all times friendly and needed assistance to said Engineer to facilitate such erection and operation.

GUARANTEE OF DUTY UPON TEST. When properly installed the Company guarantees that at a test to be conducted at the time and in the manner hereinafter set forth the machinery herein specified will operate successfully as follows:

....
....
....
....
....

which guarantees are hereinafter designated and referred to as Guarantees of Duty.

TEST. The test shall be made only if requested by the purchaser, and such request, if made, must be made immediately upon completion of installation and shall consist of......................

days' operation thereof. The said test shall be conducted at the expense of the Purchaser, by the Engineer of the Company, who shall have entire charge thereof. The Purchaser shall furnish the load necessary for such test, also a careful and competent Engineer and other labor, if required, also fuel, water, waste, lights and other incidentals needed for a proper test, rendering at all times friendly and needed assistance. The Engineer of the Company shall instruct Purchaser's Engineer in regard to the proper management and operation of the machinery. The Engineer of the Purchaser and all other help shall be under the direction of the Engineer of the Company. During erection and such test the Engineer of the Company shall be considered to be the agent of the Purchaser, and his use and possession of such machinery shall be considered to be the use and possession of the Purchaser.

If at the end of said............days' test the machinery successfully operates in accordance with the said Guarantees of Duty herein above set forth, the Purchaser shall give to the Engineer of the Company, a written acknowledgment that a successful test has been made, demonstrating that said machinery will operate successfully as provided in said Guarantee of Duty. Should the Engineer of the Company be required to remain longer than the period of such test, through any fault of the Purchaser, the Purchaser shall pay the extra time of such Engineer, at the rate of $...... per day and all expenses.

If at the end of such test, or at such time as the Company claims that said machinery has operated as provided in said Guarantees of Duty, the Purchaser fails or refuses to give such written acknowledgment that a successful test has been made, then the Purchaser shall immediately notify the Company at its office in.... ...., by registered letter, in what particulars the Purchaser claims said machinery to be defective or deficient, within said Guarantees of Duty, and the Company shall have a reasonable time after the receipt of such notification from the Purchaser, to remedy such defects or deficiencies claimed to exist. If it shall appear to be beyond the power of the Company to make the machinery perform according to said Guarantee of Duty within a reasonable time, then the Company shall remove the machinery, at no expense to the Purchaser, within a reasonable time, after giving thirty days' notice to the Purchaser, the Company having refunded to the Purchaser all purchase money paid thereon, whereupon all obligation and liability of either of the parties hereto to the other shall cease and determine and this agreement shall thereby become null and void.

It is further agreed that the use of said machinery for ten (10) days by the Purchaser after the time specified for said notice of defects as above provided, without giving notice, shall constitute an acknowledgment that said machinery has performed in strict accordance with said guarantee.

It is understood that said Guarantees of Duty are specifically limited to the operation of said machinery at a test conducted by the Engineer of the Company at the time and in the manner above set forth and that if no test be requested by the Purchaser or if such test cannot be properly conducted through any fault of the Purchaser, then said Guarantees of Duty shall be null and void and the Company not bound thereby.

GUARANTEE OF MATERIAL AND WORKMANSHIP. The machinery and materials herein specified are guaranteed by the Company to be well made of good material and in a workmanlike manner. If any parts of said machinery herein proposed to be furnished or hereafter furnished in compliance with the provisions of this paragraph, fail through defect in workmanship or material, within one year from the date of shipment thereof respectively, the Company shall replace such defective parts, free of charge, f. o. b. cars its factory, but the Company shall not be liable for repairs or alterations unless the same are made with its written consent and approval. The Company shall not be liable for damages or delays caused by such defective material or workmanship and it is agreed that, excepting its obligation to remove said machinery in the event of its inability to make said machinery operate at the test as hereinabove described according to said Guarantees of Duty, the liability of the Company under all guarantees either express or implied, is specifically limited to the replacement free of charge f. o. b. its factory of parts failing through defect in workmanship or materials within the time and in the manner aforesaid. Parts claimed to be defective are to be returned by the Purchaser to the Company at its option, transportation prepaid.

PRICES. The Company proposes to furnish said machinery and materials specified herein for the sum of......................
($............) dollars, to be paid the Company at its office in....
........................as follows:

TERMS, $...........................cash with order.
   $...........................when machinery or materials are ready for shipment.
   $...........................upon shipment, sight draft with bill of lading attached.

Balance,..
....
....

All deferred payments are to be evidenced by negotiable notes of the Purchaser payable to the order of the Company, dated and delivered as of the date of shipment and shall bear interest from said date at the rate of............per cent per annum.

This proposal is made upon the following conditions:

TITLE. That the title and ownership of the machinery or materials herein specified shall remain in the Company until final payment therefor has been made in full as above provided, and in event that notes are taken at any time, representing deferred payments, or any balance that may be due, or in the event that any judgment is taken on account of all or any part of the purchase price, the title to such machinery or materials shall not pass until such notes, so given, or extensions thereof, or such judgment taken, are fully paid in money and satisfied. The Company shall have the right to discount or transfer any of said notes, and the title or right of possession in and to said machinery or materials shall pass thereby to the legal holder of such notes.

The Purchaser shall take all such legal steps as may be required by law for the preservation of the Company's title as herein provided and in the event of default by the Purchaser in making any of said payments when due as above provided, the full amount of the purchase price shall, at the election of the Company, become immediately due and payable, in which event the Company, or its agents or representatives, shall have the right to take possession of said machinery or materials, wherever found, without process of law, and shall not be held liable for such seizure, and the Company may, at its election, upon written notice to the Purchaser, deposited in the mails ten (10) days prior thereto, addressed to the Purchaser at his last known address, sell said machinery and materials or any part thereof, at public or private sale and at which sale it shall be optional with the Company to bid for and purchase said machinery or materials or any part thereof. The Company shall retain so much of the proceeds of such sale necessary to satisfy the balance remaining due, together with the cost of such removal and sale, and any excess shall be paid to the Purchaser. Should the proceeds of such sale not cover the balance remaining due the Company, together with the cost of removal and sale, the Purchaser shall pay the deficiency to the Company forthwith after such sale. The said machinery or materials shall be and remain strictly personal property and retain its character as such, no matter whether on permanent foundation or in what manner affixed or attached to any building or structure, or what may be the consequences of its being disturbed on such foundation, building or structure, or for what purpose the machinery or materials may be used. If the Company finds it necessary to place the balance of the purchase price due and unpaid in the hands of an attorney for collection, the Purchaser shall pay in addition to said balance remaining unpaid, ten per cent (10%) thereof for the cost of the collection thereof, whether suit is filed or not.

INSURANCE. The Purchaser shall receive the machinery or materials herein specified promptly and pay all freight or other charges thereon. The Purchaser shall promptly on arrival insure such machinery or materials against loss or damage by fire in the amount remaining unpaid to the Company, in such companies satisfactory to the Company and will continue such insurance in force until the amount of such indebtedness to the Company is fully paid, loss, if any, being made payable to the Company as its interest may appear. Said policies shall be delivered to the Company at its election. Should the Purchaser fail so to do, the Company may obtain such insurance at the Purchaser's expense. In case of loss or damage by fire, such loss or damage shall have the effect of immediately assigning said insurance to the Company, whether or not taken out for its benefit. The Purchaser shall make good any loss to the Company by reason of any damage to said machinery or materials caused by fire, carelessness or other injuries.

RESPONSIBILITY FOR DELAYS. The Company shall not be liable for any damage due to delay in transportation or delay in shipment caused by strikes, fires, floods, combination of labor, or other causes beyond its control and the receipt of said machinery or materials by the Purchaser shall constitute a waiver of any claim for damage due to delay. Should the Purchaser decline to receive said machinery or materials upon its arrival, the damages for delay in filling or shipping the same shall in no event exceed in amount the rental value of similar machinery or materials for the period of such delay which is agreed to be the sole measure of such damage. The Purchaser shall pay to the Company twenty (20%) per cent of the purchase price stated in this proposal as agreed liquidated damages, if before shipment, the Purchaser countermands this proposal. After shipment there can be no countermand on the part of the Purchaser.

This proposal is binding when signed by the Purchaser and approved by an executive officer of the Company. This proposal is executed in duplicate and it is expressly understood that it contains all of the agreements between the parties hereto, pertaining to said machinery or materials herein specified and that there is no verbal understanding whatever between the parties hereto in reference thereto.

The Company shall not be held responsible for damages of any character arising by the use of said machinery or materials either original or consequential, it being specifically agreed that the liability of the Company is specifically limited as hereinabove set forth.

Respectfully submitted,

....

(Salesman National Machinery Co.)

The above proposal is hereby accepted this............day of
................19...

With the definite understanding that there are no verbal agreements or understandings changing or modifying it.

Witness..............................
Witness..............................

If Purchaser is a corporation } Signed by ....
....
....

Approved.................. NATIONAL MACHINERY CO.,
By.......................

Routing Instructions..
Ship to..
Via..

NOTE.—The foregoing type of contract is on an entirely different theory than the one preceding it, and involves an entire change in sales policy. This form, quoted above, involves a definite guarantee of duty upon the part of the seller, but positively limits the seller's liability, in the event that he is unable to comply with the guarantee, to taking back the machinery and refunding the purchase price. It very strictly provides, however, that the purchaser is positively bound by an acceptance if he uses the machinery for ten days after the time specified for notice of defects, and if defects are claimed they must be stipulated in a registered communication addressed to the company immediately after the test provided for is made by the seller's engineers or immediately after the time provided for a test even if none is conducted.

SHORT ORDER FORM, CONDITIONAL SALE CONTRACT, FOR SALESMEN

....
Salesman. } ORDER No. ....

Original

.... 19..
National Machinery & Supply Co.,......................
Charge to...
Address..
Ship to..
Via..

Purchase Price $..
Payable as follows $............Cash with order, $.............
Cash upon shipment, Balance $.................................

from date of shipment, without any deduction for Freight, Express or Exchange Charges. Deferred payments to be evidenced by negotiable notes bearing.................... % interest per annum from date. It is agreed that title and ownership of above described property shall remain in National Machinery & Supply Co., until fully paid for. In case Purchaser does not make payment as agreed, National Machinery & Supply Co., may, at their option, remove property, wherever found, without process of law, and sell same after ten days' notice to Purchaser, applying proceeds first on balance due and any remaining after expenses of sale have been paid, to be turned over to Purchaser. Should the proceeds of such sale not cover the balance remaining due National Machinery & Supply Co., together with the cost of removal and sale, Purchaser shall pay the deficiency to National Machinery & Supply Co., forthwith after such sale. Purchaser also agrees to pay National Machinery & Supply Co., 20% of the net amount stated in this order as agreed liquidated damages in event this order is countermanded. All orders are contingent upon and subject to strikes, accidents and other causes beyond the control of National Machinery & Supply Co. It is expressly understood that there are no verbal understandings pertaining to the above. This order is taken subject to the approval of the local manager of National Machinery & Supply Co. Approved .... 19... The order has been read NATIONAL MACHINERY & SUPPLY Co. by the undersigned and By................................ acknowledged to be correct.

Signed

....
(*Purchaser sign here*)

CONDITIONAL CONTRACT OF SALE

I. Walter Johnson, of Albany, New York, have this day received from the National Sewing Machine Company, of New York City, New York, the following described property: One National Sewing Machine No. 18768, drop cabinet,............................
....
the value of which is hereby fixed at sixty dollars ($60.00), under the following agreement of conditional sale:

APPENDIX

I hereby agree to pay the National Sewing Machine Company the sum of five dollars ($5.00) cash on signing this contract and the further sum of one dollar each week thereafter, on Saturday of each week, at the First National Bank in Albany, New York, until I have paid the full amount of sixty dollars ($60.00).

When I shall have paid the full amount hereinbefore provided for, I am to have title and ownership to said property, the said National Sewing Machine Company to have title and ownership therein until all payments have been made in full.

I expressly agree to use the aforesaid property, during the life of this contract, in a careful manner; and I agree not to remove said property from the premises I now occupy without first obtaining the written consent of said National Sewing Machine Company.

On default by me in any payment, covenant or agreement herein provided for, the National Sewing Machine Company may, without notice to me, enter my premises where the aforesaid property is located, take immediate and full possession thereof, and after holding the same in any manner for thirty (30) days, all my rights therein or to the possession thereof or to payments made thereon shall cease absolutely, without notice of any subsequent private or public sale; and I hereby waive all claim for damages or otherwise against said National Sewing Machine Company on account of any removal or attempted removal of aforesaid property.

I hereby agree to pay any and all charges, expenses and attorneys' or collectors' fees incurred in taking possession of the aforesaid property or in collecting any balance due from me hereunder.

IN WITNESS WHEREOF, I have hereunto subscribed my name to this agreement in duplicate, on this............day of.........., 1918, one copy of which was delivered to and retained by me.

....
(*Purchaser*).

Accepted:
NATIONAL SEWING MACHINE CO.,

Witnesses:

By ....

....
....

INDEX

(A)

	Page
Adjustment Bureaus	145
Application for Extension, form of	59
Arbitration, commercial	141
Assignment of open accounts	131

(B)

Bankruptcy	152
Banks, form of inquiry to	41
Blank check, form of	136
Blank check, use of	135
Bureaus of Adjustment	145
Bankruptcy, U. S. Law	175

(a)

Accounts and papers of Trustees	226
Acts of bankruptcy	187
Appeals and writs of error	209
Appointment of Trustees	220
Appointment, removal and districts of Referees	214
Arbitration of controversies	210

(b)

Bankruptcy, definition of	179
Bonds of Referees	226
Bonds of Trustees	226

(c)

Claims, proof and allowance of	233
Co-debtors of bankrupts	200
Compensation of clerks	229

294 INDEX

	PAGE
Compensation of Marshals	223
Compensation of Receivers	223
Compensation of Trustees	223
Compensation of Referee	218
Compositions, when confirmed	196
Compositions, when set aside	198
Compromises	211
Computation of time	213
Contempts before Referee	218
Courts of Bankruptcy, creation of	183
Creation of Two Offices	214

(d)

Death or removal of Trustee	221
Death or insanity of bankrupts	194
Debtors not affected by discharge	200
Debts which may be proved	241
Definitions	179
Depositories of money	241
Designation of newspapers	211
Discharges, when granted	198
Discharges, when revoked	200
Dividends, declaration of	244
Dividends, payment of	245
Dividends, unclaimed	246
Duties of Attorney General	230
Duties of bankrupts	192
Duties of clerks	228
Duties of Referee	216
Duties of Trustee	221

(e)

Effect on partnership	190
Evidence	205
Exemption of bankrupts	192
Expenses of administering estates	241
Extradition of bankrupts	195

INDEX

(j)

	Page
Jurisdiction of Appellate Courts	208
Jurisdiction of Bankruptcy Courts	184
Jurisdiction of Referee	215
Jurisdiction of U. S. and State Courts	207
Jury Trials	203

(l)

Liens	246

(m)

Meaning of words and phrases	179
Meetings of creditors	231

(n)

Notice to creditors	236
Number of Referees	215

(o)

Oaths, affirmation	204
Oaths of Office of Referee	215
Offenses	211

(p)

Possession of property	250
Preferred creditors	239
Process, Pleadings and Adjudications	202
Protection and detention of bankrupts	194

(q)

Qualifications of Referees	214
Qualifications of Trustees	221

(r)

Records of Referees	219
Referee's absence or disability	220

	PAGE
Reference of cases after adjudication	207
Rules, forms and orders	213

(s)

Set-offs and counterclaims	249
Statistics of bankruptcy proceedings	230
Suits by and against bankrupts	196

(t)

Time of effect of act	254
Title to property	251
Transfer of cases	213

(v)

Voters at meetings of creditors	232

(w)

Who may become bankrupts	190
Who may file and dismiss petitions	237

(C)

Checks on blank form	136
Collateral note, form of	128
Collection Agencies	148
Collection Agency, organizing your own	164
Collectors, function of	107
Commercial Arbitration	141
Compiling information, method of	46
Conditional Sales Contracts	82
Conditional Sales Contracts, general exceptions to validity of	83
Conditional Sales Contracts, (Engine form)	281
Conditional Sales Contracts, (Machinery form)	277
Conditional Sales Contracts, (Salesman short order form)	289
Conditional Sales Contracts, (Sewing Machines)	290
Conditional Sales Contracts, (Short form)	273

INDEX

	PAGE
Conditional Sales Contracts, (Simple form)	274
Conditional Sales Contracts, (Pennsylvania Lease form)	275
Contracts, Conditional Sales	82
Converting doubtful orders	66
Co-operation	52
Creating offsets	138
Credit Statement	40–41
Credit System	3
Credits—fixing limits	47
Credits—laws relating to	98
Crop reports	102

Conditional Sales Contracts—Requirements of States:

Alabama	255
Arizona	255
Arkansas	256
California	256
Colorado	256
Connecticut	256
Delaware	257
District of Columbia	257
Florida	257
Georgia	258
Idaho	258
Illinois	259
Indiana	259
Iowa	259
Kansas	260
Kentucky	260
Louisiana	260
Maine	261
Maryland	261
Massachusetts	261
Michigan	262
Minnesota	262
Mississippi	262
Missouri	263

	PAGE
Montana	264
Nebraska	264
Nevada	264
New Hampshire	265
New Jersey	265
New Mexico	265
New York	266
North Carolina	266
North Dakota	266
Ohio	267
Oklahoma	267
Oregon	267
Pennsylvania	268
Rhode Island	268
South Carolina	268
South Dakota	269
Tennessee	269
Texas	269
Utah	270
Vermont	270
Virginia	270
Washington	271
West Virginia	271
Wisconsin	271
Wyoming	272

(D)

Debtors, tracing lost	139
Declined orders, record of	47
Diplomacy	52
Doubtful orders, converting	66

(E)

Elements of preferences	160
Extension, form of application for	59
Engine form, Conditional Sales Contract	281

(F)

	PAGE
Farmers, report on from salesmen	28
Fixing credit limits	47
Follow up system collections	114
Form of application for extension of payment	59
Form of blank check	136
Form of collateral note	128
Form of conditional sales contract (Engines)	281
Form of conditional sales contract (Machinery)	277
Form of conditional sales contract (Penn. Lease form)	275
Form of conditional sales contract (Sewing Machines)	291
Form of conditional sales contract (Short)	273
Form of conditional sales contract (Shortorders, salesmanform)	289
Form of conditional sales contract (Simple)	274
Form of guarantee (before shipment)	70
Form of guarantee (on past due accounts)	73
Form of individual statements	40–41
Form of inquiry to banks	41
Form of inquiry to other merchants	42
Form of report on farmers (Salesman)	28
Form of report on manufacturers (Salesman)	27
Form of report on merchants (Salesman)	20
Form of report on mining companies (Salesman)	36
Form of report on oil producers (Salesman)	31
Forms of mercantile credit	4
Form of promissory note	125
Functions of collectors	107
Functions of credit man	12
Fundamental principles of credit	7

(G)

General knowledge of law	97
Guarantee form, before shipment	70
Guarantee form, on past due accounts	73

(I)

Implied warranties	100
Incorporating your own collection agency	165

	PAGE
Indiana form of incorporation (collection agency)	167
Individual statement—form of	40–41
Information—method of compiling	46
Inquiry blank to banks	41
Inquiry blank form to other merchants	42

(K)

Knowledge of law	97

(L)

Law, general knowledge of	97
Laws relating to credits	98
Lost debtors, tracing	139

(M)

Machinery, form of conditional sales contract	277
Manufacturers, report on from salesman	27
Merchants, report on from salesman	20
Merchants, form of inquiry to	42
Method of compiling information	46
Mining companies, report on from salesman	36

(N)

Names for your own collection agency	168
New York form of incorporation of collection agencies	165

(O)

Offsets, creating	138
Oil Producers, report on from salesman	31
Open accounts, form of assignment of	131

(P)

Payment, form of guarantee before shipment	70
Payment, form of guarantee open account	73
Pennsylvania Lease form, conditional sales contract	275
Preferences, elements of	160

INDEX

	PAGE
Preferences in bankruptcy	158
Promissory note, collateral form	128
Promissory note, form of	125
Property statement—individual form	40–41
Protest, waiver of	125

(R)

Reading financial statement	75
Record of declined orders	47
Report on farmers, from salesman	28
Report on manufacturers, from salesman	27
Report on merchants, from salesman	20
Report on mining companies, from salesman	36
Report on oil producers, from salesman	31
Reports—crop	102
Resourceful methods	121

(S)

Sales contracts, conditional	82
Salesman's report form—farmers	28
Salesman's report form—manufacturers	27
Salesman's report form—merchants	20
Salesman's report form—mining companies	36
Salesman's report form—oil producers	31
Selecting a Trustee in bankruptcy	157
Sewing Machine form—conditional sales contract	290
Short form, conditional sales contract	273
Short form, conditional sales contract (Salesman's order blank)	289
Simple form, conditional sales contract	274
Source of information—direct	19
Statement—individual form	40–41

(T)

Tracing lost debtors	139
Trade acceptances	89
Trustee in bankruptcy—selecting	157

	PAGE
(U)	
Use of blank checks	135
(W)	
Waiver of protest	125
Warranties, Implied	100
(Y)	
Your own collection agency—organizing	164
Your own collection agency—incorporating	165
Your own collection agency—naming	168

Printed in the United States of America

THE following pages contain advertisements of a few of the Macmillan books on kindred subjects

A NEW IDEA IN INDUSTRY

The Shop Committee
A HAND-BOOK FOR EMPLOYERS AND EMPLOYEES
By WILLIAM LEAVITT STODDARD, A.B., A.M.,
HARVARD

Administrator for the National War Labor Board, 1918–1919

Cloth, 12mo, $1.25

The Shop Committee is a new thing in industry. Here is a clear statement of the essential principles and facts of the Shop Committee System, what it is and how it works. Every large employer will be vitally interested in this new industrial movement, described for the first time in Mr. Stoddard's book.

TABLE OF CONTENTS

CHAPTER

I—The Early Beginnings: History of the shop committee movement in this country and Great Britain with particular reference to the developments since the war and shop committees as a reconstruction measure.

II—The War Labor Board Plan: Development of shop committees by the National War Labor Board, describing particularly the Pittsfield, Mass., plan (General Electric Co.).

III—General Principles: An analysis of the underlying principles of collective bargaining through shop committees.

IV—The Basis of Representation: Discussion in detail and with practical illustrations of the districting or dividing of a plant into shops, districts, and other units of self-government. Shows common errors into which employers and employees fall.

V—The Lynn Plan: Shop Committee Scheme of the Lynn, Mass., Plant. (General Electric Co.).

VI—Three Characteristic Plans: Describes plan installed in Pittsfield Machine and Tool Co., Pittsfield, Mass. Also plan at Bridgeport, Conn., and Philadelphia (Rapid Transit Co.).

VII—Election Machinery: Similar to Chapter IV, a practical, detailed discussion of how to hold elections.

VIII—Procedure: Similar to IV and VII.

IX—Shop Committees in Action: Stories and actual incidents related.

X—The Shop Committee and the Union: Important discussion of this question with particular reference to whether the formation of shop committees promotes unions or not.

THE MACMILLAN COMPANY
Publishers   64–66 Fifth Avenue   New York

JULIUS HENRY COHEN'S NEW BOOK

An American Labor Policy

Cloth, 12mo, $1.00

Mr. Julius Henry Cohen, whose previous work, "Law and Order in Industry" received much favorable comment, gives in this new volume a compact and well-defined presentation of a definite Labor Policy.

Law and Order in Industry

By JULIUS HENRY COHEN

Cloth, 12mo, $1.50

A lawyer who knows the facts of the case from intimate knowledge gives in this book a comprehensive story of the "Protocol" experiences in the cloak and suit industry of New York. He describes vividly the processes and results of collective dealing between a trades union and an employers' association covering a period of five years. The solution of the apparently baffling problems furnishes lessons of great immediate and future import to all employers of labor, trades unionists, social reformers and students of political science and economics.

"The book is a distinct contribution to the science of social relations and as such should have a wide reading both here and abroad."—*The Independent*.

"His book is a sound and reliable study of a small, but significant, phase of a world-wide movement."
—*Boston Daily Advertiser*.

THE MACMILLAN COMPANY
Publishers   64–66 Fifth Avenue   New York

History of Labor in the United States
By JOHN R. COMMONS
Professor of Political Economy, University of Wisconsin, President American Economic Association.
With collaborators

In two Vols. 8°, $6.50

"The fullest and most careful history of labor in the United States that has yet appeared."—*The New York Evening Post.*

"It will doubtless be generally accepted as the standard history of American labor."—*The New York Tribune.*

"A monumental study . . . this probably is the final history of labor in our country during the centuries which immediately precede our own times."—*The New York Times.*

Labor and Administration
By JOHN R. COMMONS
Cloth, 12mo, $1.60

"Straightforward and fearless examinations of fact."—*Boston Evening Transcript.*

"There is not a chapter which does not contain information which is practical and timely."—*San Francisco Chronicle.*

"Each chapter is a book in itself worthy of careful perusal. . . . Written in his unusual vivid and interesting style."—*Post Dispatch, St. Louis.*

An Introduction to the Study of Organized Labor in America
By GEORGE GORHAM GROAT
Professor of Economics in the University of Vermont

$1.90

"Those interested in the study of the labor movement in this country will find Professor Groat's book exceedingly helpful—a singularly fair presentation of labor's problem."—*San Francisco Bulletin.*

"His volume is admirably adapted to giving the student a conception of the swiftly changing currents in the field of organized labor."—*New York Evening Post.*

THE MACMILLAN COMPANY
Publishers   64–66 Fifth Avenue   New York

The Labor Market

By DON D. LESCOHIER

Cloth, 12°

The employment problem analyzed as a market problem, including a careful study of the factors which influence supply and demand of labor in normal times and the effect of war upon the labor market.

Workmen's Compensation

By J. E. RHODES, 2ND

Cloth, 8vo, $1.50

A history of the Workmen's Compensation movement in this country, and an outline of the principles on which the system is based.

War Time Control of Industry

By HOWARD L. GRAY

Cloth, 12°, $1.75

A review of England's problem of government control during the war is particularly significant in the light of the present condition in our own country.

THE MACMILLAN COMPANY
Publishers   64–66 Fifth Avenue   New York